Army Air Forces Historical Studies: No. 34

ARMY AIR FORCES in the WAR AGAINST JAPAN
1941 – 1942

———— Prepared by ————
ASSISTANT CHIEF OF AIR STAFF
INTELLIGENCE
HISTORICAL DIVISION

ARMY AIR FORCES HISTORICAL STUDIES: NO. 34

ARMY AIR FORCES

IN THE WAR AGAINST JAPAN

1941-1942

The original of this monograph and the documents from which it was written are in the USAF Historical Division, Archives Branch, bldg. 914, Maxwell Air Force Base, Alabama.

Prepared by
Assistant Chief of Air Staff, Intelligence
Historical Division
June 1945

FOREWORD

This narrative, prepared by the Historical Division, AC/AS, Intelligence provides a factual account of AAF combat operations during the earliest phase of the war against Japan. It does not pretend to tell the full story, which at this time or within this compass is impossible, and the account is subject to revision as additional information becomes available. It is based, however, upon careful research, having been drawn for the most part from fully documented studies prepared by the Historical Division and from materials forwarded by historical officers of the several air forces. The primary purpose has been to provide for personnel of the Army Air Forces a ready reference to useful information.

CONTENTS

ON THE DEFENSIVE

I.	Prologue	1
II.	The Hawaiian Air Force at Pearl Harbor	8
III.	The Far East Air Force in the Philippines	20
IV	Defense of the Netherlands East Indies	45
V.	Withdrawal to Australia	66
VI.	Air Reinforcements for the Asiatic Mainland	92
VII.	The Tokyo Raid	106

THE CRISIS OF MAY AND JUNE

I	The Allied Air Forces—Coral Sea	110
II	The Seventh Air Force—Midway	113
III.	The Eleventh Air Force—Dutch Harbor	121

LIMITED OFFENSIVES

I	Guadalcanal and Origins of the Thirteenth Air Force	128
II.	The Fifth Air Force in New Guinea	142
III	The Eleventh Air Force in the Aleutians	161
IV	The Tenth Air Force in India and China	169
V	Epilogue	183
	INDEX	186

MAPS

Pacific Air Forces, 7 December 1941	Frontispiece
The Philippine Islands	21
Air Routes to the Far East	48
The ABDA Area	53
Australia and Related Areas	68
Pacific Ocean Areas, May 1942	78
India-China Ferry Routes, 1942	95
The Aleutian Islands	122
The Solomons and Related Areas	130
The Solomon Islands	136
Southeastern New Guinea	147
Pacific Air Forces, December 1942	182

I

PROLOGUE

The combat story of the AAF during the first year of the war against Japan is essentially an account of a struggle against odds-- against numerically superior enemy forces, against shortages of planes, spare parts, repair facilities, trained aircrews, ground personnel, and aircraft warning facilities, and against time itself. In comparison with later efforts the operations were both meager and sporadic, but they were nonetheless significant. During the final weeks of 1941 and the early months of 1942 Allied forces suffered one reverse after another, as Japanese air, ground, and naval forces swept over vast areas with relative ease and almost unbelievable speed. In attempting to halt the onrush the air arm carried an especially heavy burden. The unique capabilities of its weapons enabled the AAF to reach out and strike at the enemy ~~long~~ before sizable ground and naval forces could be brought into battle. When the crucial test came at mid-year, the AAF shared with the Navy the honor of turning back the enemy's advance, and before the year's end its planes had inaugurated limited offensives in China, New Guinea, the Solomons, and the Aleutians.

At the outbreak of hostilities the AAF had outside continental United States a total of 913 aircraft--636 fighters and 61 heavy, 157 medium, and 59 light bombers--divided among Panama, Puerto Rico, Trinidad, the Virgin Islands, British Guiana, the Windward Islands,

Newfoundland, Greenland, Iceland, Alaska, Hawaii, and the Philippines. An unprecedented program of expansion, undertaken in the face of a European war and mounting tension in the Pacific, had imposed a heavy strain upon air facilities and organizations. But despite attendant difficulties, reinforcements were being rushed to American outposts as rapidly as the availability of men and planes permitted, with special attention directed to requirements for the Pacific.

Alaska

In Alaska, the Air Force, Alaska Defense Command* was both the smallest and the youngest of overseas air forces. Had the Japanese chosen to attack the naval base at Dutch Harbor in the Aleutians on 7 December 1941, they would have met no opposition from Army planes, for on that day only 6 B-18's and 12 P-36's could be put into the air at Elmendorf Field, 1,000 miles to the east at Anchorage. The development of military and naval installations in Alaska had been a slow process. Construction of Elmendorf Field had not begun until 1940, and the first Air Corps units began moving from the United States to Elmendorf early in 1941. The 23d Air Base Group, the 18th Pursuit Squadron, and the 28th Composite Group, composed of the Headquarters and Headquarters Squadron, the 36th Bombardment Squadron (H), and the 73d Bombardment Squadron (H), had all arrived by the end of March.

Though for a time its planes were limited to a few B-18's and P-36's, by December there were indications that the air force in

* So designated on 17 October, having been formed as the Air Field Forces, Alaska Defense Command on 29 May 1941.

Alaska would soon be able to provide effective air defense of the area. Under the leadership of Brig. Gen. Simon B. Buckner, Jr., the Alaska Defense Command was beginning to implement plans for an airfield at Umnak in the Aleutians, 65 miles west of Dutch Harbor, and for a series of staging fields connecting it with the main base at Anchorage. And while the scarcity of Air Corps personnel and equipment in the United States would not permit immediate enlargement of the Alaskan air force, arrangements had been made for units of the Fourth Air Force to be shifted to Alaska in case of invasion or other emergency.

Hawaii

In the Territory of Hawaii, the Hawaiian Air Force, under the command of Maj. Gen. Frederick L. Martin, had a total strength of 754 officers and 6,706 enlisted men. Its 231 aircraft of all types were based on the island of Oahu, site of Pearl Harbor Naval Base. At Hickam Field were the 5th and 11th Bombardment Groups (comprising the 18th Bombardment Wing), the 17th Air Base Group, the 19th Transport Squadron, maintenance companies, and other detachments. Wheeler Field was the station for the 15th Air Base Group, and the 14th Pursuit Wing, composed of the 15th and 18th Pursuit Groups and necessary attached services. The 86th Observation Squadron was located at Bellows Field, on the southeastern end of the island. A small field at Haleiwa, to the northwest, was being used in training pursuit squadrons, while additional fields were being constructed on other islands of the Hawaiian group.

South Pacific Air Route

Notable in efforts to strengthen America's Pacific garrisons had been the first flights of B-17's to Hawaii and the Philippines. On 13 May 1941 the 19th Bombardment Group had ferried 21 B-17's in the initial mass flight of Flying Fortresses to Hickam Field from Hamilton Field, Calif. The crews remained in Hawaii for approximately 2 weeks in order to check off members of the 11th Bombardment Group on the B-17. Success of this flight pointed to the more ambitious undertaking of flying heavy bombers to the Philippines, and by the close of summer a military air route had been prepared from Hawaii, by way of Midway, Wake, and Australian territory, to the Philippine Islands. The vulnerability of this route across Japanese-mandated islands gave special urgency to an Air Corps project, authorized in October, for a South Pacific route by way of Christmas and Canton Islands, the Fijis, and New Caledonia to Australia and thence to Luzon. Responsibility for development of the route, which was not completed until after the opening of hostilities, was divided between the commanding generals of the Hawaiian Department and of the U. S. Army Forces in the Far East.

Philippines

When war came to the Philippines, the Far East Air Force under Maj. Gen. Lewis H. Brereton had been built into the largest of the overseas air forces--8,000 officers and men and more than 300 aircraft, concentrated largely on the island of Luzon. But less than half of these aircraft were suitable for combat, and much of the necessary equipment was still awaiting shipment from the United States. Preparations for defense of the Islands were going forward rapidly under the direction of Gen. Douglas C. MacArthur, former chief of staff of the U. S. Army and military adviser to the Philippine government. During the summer of 1941 General MacArthur had been recalled to active duty and on 26 July placed in command of U. S. Army Forces in the Far East. A new emphasis on air defense was reflected in the increase in tactical units, the provision of more modern equipment, organizational changes, and an extensive program of airfield construction.

One year prior to the outbreak of hostilities there were only three major military airfields in the Philippines--Clark Field, about 60 miles north of Manila, and Nichols and Nielson fields on the outskirts of Manila. Of these, only Clark was suitable for use by heavy bombers. On Mindanao Island, in the southern Philippines, construction was soon begun on Del Monte Field, which was to be large enough to accommodate heavy bombers. By the first of December 1941, three additional fields on Luzon were being used by pursuit planes, four more fields were nearing completion, and work had been started on a number of others.

On 6 May the one medium bombardment squadron, one observation squadron, and three pursuit squadrons representing the Air Corps in the Philippines had been organized into the Philippine Department Air Force.* In the same month the pursuit squadrons began to receive P-35's

---

*/ Redesignated on 4 August 1941 as the Air Forces, U. S. Army Forces in the Far East.

as replacements for their outmoded P-26's, and during the summer and fall a limited number of P-40B's and P-40E's arrived. On 16 September these pursuit squadrons were organized into the 24th Pursuit Group and placed under the command of Maj. Orrin L. Grover. An increase in bombardment and service units having brought about further changes in the air force, it became the Far East Air Force on 28 October. A reorganization effective 16 November 1941 resulted in disbandment of the 4th Composite Group and activation of the V Bomber Command and the Far East Service Command.

The first heavy bombers had arrived in September, when Maj. Emmett O'Donnell, Jr., led nine B-17's of the 14th Bombardment Squadron from Hickam Field via the northern route to Clark Field. Two months later 26 additional B-17's were flown from the United States over the same route by crews of the 19th Bombardment Group under the command of Lt. Col. Eugene L. Eubank. In November two more pursuit squadrons and the 27th Bombardment Group (L) arrived by water. The 27th Group, under the command of Maj. John H. Davies, had been forced to leave its 52 A-24's in the United States for shipment in a later convoy, while a last-minute change of orders kept its 15th Squadron in the States. The 7th Bombardment Group (H) was under orders to move to the Philippines, and the first week of December 1941 found most of its ground echelon en route in a convoy which carried also the A-24's of the 27th Group.

But the course of events did not allow these and other projected reinforcements to reach their destination. As a result, the Army's air defense of the Philippines had to be provided by one heavy bombardment group with 35 B-17's, one light bombardment group with no planes, one pursuit group with 90 operational P-40's, one Philippine squadron equipped with 12 old P-26's, and one observation squadron with a miscellaneous assortment of 21 planes.

In the Philippines, as in Alaska, on Oahu, and along the partially completed South Pacific route, the AAF was preparing against the day when the inevitable would come, but that day came with devastating suddenness.

II
THE HAWAIIAN AIR FORCE AT PEARL HARBOR

When diplomatic relations between Japan and the United States neared the breaking point in November 1941, both the War and Navy Departments notified their commanders in outlying territories and possessions. Procedures had been agreed upon in Hawaii for the use of Army and Navy air forces in case of an air attack, and during 1941 frequent drills and maneuvers had tested these procedures. It was believed by commanding officers and their staffs that there was little chance of an air raid on Oahu while the Pacific Fleet was in Pearl Harbor. If such an attack were made, it was felt that dawn would be the most likely time of occurrence. Upon receipt of warnings from the War and Navy Departments, forces in the Territory of Hawaii were placed on an alert. A temporary aircraft warning system, which was being used pending the completion of permanent installations, was ordered on 27 November to be placed in operation from 0400 to 0700 daily.

The type of alert under which the Army and Navy forces were operating placed major emphasis on the prevention of subversive acts, for an estimate of the situation indicated that in Oahu sabotage was more likely than an enemy attack. To protect aircraft, planes were concentrated in hangars or in open spaces nearby. Extra guards were placed about the aircraft and around certain military installations.

Construction was started on protective fencing and flood-lighting projects.

It remained for the events of 7 December 1941 to prove that the island of Oahu was subject to a danger far greater than that of sabotage. At 0630 on that Sunday morning the U. S. S. *Antares* sighted a suspicious object in the restricted area off Pearl Harbor. The object was discovered to be a small submarine, which was attacked and sunk within 15 minutes by joint action of the U. S. S. *Ward* and a naval patrol plane. At 0712 the naval base watch officer received a report of this action and relayed the report to his chief of staff. No alert warnings were issued, although a destroyer was dispatched to investigate the incident.

In accordance with the order from the commanding general of the Hawaiian Department, all six detector stations of the Hawaiian Interceptor Command were in operation from 0400 to 0700. In addition to the watch officer, a plotting detail of one noncommissioned officer and 10 enlisted men was on duty at the information center which had been set up in a temporary installation near Fort Shafter. At 0700 all detector stations closed with the exception of the Opana Station at Kahuku Point, which remained open in order to continue training a man in the operation of the oscilloscope. At 0702 the station plotted a group of airplanes at 136 miles, bearing 0° to 3°. A report was telephoned to the information center at 0720, but the watch officer did not consider it necessary to take any action because of an expected arrival of B-17's from the mainland and the probability of operations by naval aircraft. The Opana Station tracked the planes toward the island and then lost them.

Attacks on Naval Installations

Two opportunities for advance notice having passed, the forces on Oahu were completely surprised at 0755, when more than 100 Japanese carrier-based planes swarmed over the island to carry out concentrated attacks on Army and Navy installations, including Pearl Harbor and all air bases. Eight battleships, 7 cruisers, 28 destroyers, and 5 submarines were among the 86 units of the Pacific Fleet moored in the harbor. For approximately 30 minutes Japanese torpedo planes, dive bombers, and horizontal bombers bore in upon the vessels in wave after wave, leaving burning and exploding warships. During this period a total of 30 dive-bombers made eight attacks, and 21 torpedo planes attacked in four waves, with 15 horizontal bombers and several submarines also participating. Battleships, cruisers, and destroyers opened machine-gun fire almost immediately, and within a few minutes all antiaircraft batteries were in action.

Most of the planes withdrew at 0825, but 15 minutes later more bombers appeared and for half an hour carried out bombing and strafing attacks, not only on the craft in Pearl Harbor but also on all Army and Navy air facilities which had been hit in the first phase of the action. Following this series of attacks Pearl Harbor was again attacked by high-altitude horizontal bombers.

Damage to naval installations and equipment was heavy.* Five

---

* Figures on naval losses are taken from a Navy report released on 6 December 1942.

battleships, the Arizona, California, Oklahoma, Nevada, and West Virginia; 3 destroyers, the Cassin, Downes, and Shaw; 1 target ship, the Utah; 1 minelayer, the Oglala, and a large floating drydock were either sunk or damaged so severely that they were put out of action for a considerable length of time. Also damaged were 3 battleships, the Maryland, Pennsylvania, and Tennessee; 3 cruisers, the Helena, Honolulu, and Raleigh; the seaplane tender Curtiss; and the repair ship Vestal. When the first attack began, 7 naval planes were carrying out patrol missions. The attacks on Ford Island, Kaneohe Bay, and Ewa Field resulted in the permanent or temporary disabling of 150 of the 202 naval aircraft in flying condition. Of the remaining 52 planes, 38 took to the air during the day. Included in these totals are 18 scout bombing planes which took off from an aircraft carrier en route to Pearl Harbor and which arrived by chance during the raid; 4 of these bombers were lost as a result of enemy action. Losses in Naval and Marine Corps personnel were extremely heavy, with 2,117 officers and enlisted men reported killed, 960 missing, and 876 wounded. Aircraft losses could be replaced within a reasonably short time; recuperation from damage to ships would require much longer; and there could be no immediate replacement of trained personnel.

Attacks on Army Airfields

Like the action at Pearl Harbor, enemy attacks on Army airfields revealed careful planning and skillful execution in order to achieve a maximum amount of destruction. Wheeler, Hickam, and Bellows fields suffered severe losses in aircraft and installations. Before the first attack, essentially all aircraft were either in hangars or lined up in front of hangars, in accordance with the policy of affording maximum protection against possible sabotage. The type of alert then in effect required that aircraft be ready for flight only after 4 hours' notice; the planes were therefore not loaded with ammunition.

At Wheeler Field the first attack came a few minutes past 0800, when a large formation of dive-bombers flew in from the north at about 5,000 feet. The planes peeled off and at an altitude of from 500 to 1,000 feet released a total of approximately 25 bombs on the hangar line. Two hangars were hit and set on fire, along with storehouses and barracks, where a considerable number of casualties occurred. After dropping their bombs the planes came down to an extremely low altitude and strafed the aircraft parked in front of the hangars. Tracer and incendiary bullets penetrated the gasoline tanks, setting the planes afire. Ammunition was also fired into the windows of buildings. Officers and men at Wheeler Field immediately began to taxi planes out of burning hangars; they pulled undamaged planes away from burning ones, fought fires, and rescued the wounded. Shortly after 0900 seven planes made a second attack, apparently expending on Wheeler Field what ammunition was left after the second raid on Pearl Harbor and Hickam Field.

The attacks on Hickam Field conformed to the pattern of those on Wheeler. Initial dive bombing, with a high degree of accuracy, followed by strafing of buildings and parked planes, resulted in heavy damage to the Hawaiian Air Depot, as well as to the mess hall, hangars, barracks, and the B-17's, B-18's, and A-20's at the field. The destruction of repair docks and stores of supplies left only limited repair and supply facilities for the Hawaiian Air Force.

From the standpoint of the Japanese, the attacks on Army installations were highly successful. Of the 231 aircraft of all types on hand, 152 were either permanently or temporarily disabled, leaving only 79 usable after the raid. Sixteen of these planes were observation, training, or outmoded types not suitable for combat. While casualties among Army personnel were not so great in number as were those of the Navy, the 226 officers and men who were killed, along with the 396 who were wounded, represented a definite loss to the Army air and ground units on Oahu.

Army Air Action

The destruction which the Japanese brought about in their surprise assault tends to overshadow other aspects of the event, but a small number of fighter pilots took to the air and engaged the enemy with a success which belied their lack of combat experience. At about 0850 four members of the 46th Squadron of the 15th Pursuit Group took off from Wheeler Field in P-36's and were ordered to proceed at 8,000 feet to the vicinity of Diamond Head. Near Bellows Field they attacked a formation of nine Japanese aircraft. 1st Lt. Lewis M. Sanders and 2d Lt. Philip M. Rasmussen each shot down one enemy plane. 2d Lt. Gordon H. Sterling, Jr., either damaged or destroyed an enemy plane; but while doing so he was attacked from the rear and was shot down in flames. 2d Lt. John M. Thacker remained in the attack until after his guns had jammed; though hit by enemy cannon fire, the plane was returned safely to Wheeler Field. Another member of the 46th Squadron, 1st Lt. Malcolm A. Moore, took to the air and encountered an enemy plane over Kaena Point. The Japanese craft escaped into a cloud formation, but only after being hit a number of times.

The 44th Squadron of the 18th Pursuit Group was on detached service at Bellows Field for gunnery training. Notified of the attack on Wheeler Field, crews immediately began arming the planes. When Japanese aircraft appeared over the field, three pilots attempted to take off. 2d Lt. Hans C. Christiansen was killed by enemy machine gun fire while getting into a P-40. 2d Lt. George A. Whiteman managed to get his plane off the ground, but he was immediately shot down. One plane, piloted by 1st Lt. Samuel W. Bishop, engaged in combat but received damages which resulted in a crash landing in the waters nearby. In spite of a wounded leg, Lieutenant Bishop swam ashore. Low-flying enemy aircraft over Bellows Field met with gun fire from O-47's on the ground when certain enlisted men of the 86th Observation Squadron, acting without orders, dashed to the planes and mounted machine guns in the cockpits. The men continued to fire at the enemy until the attack ended.

The only usable airfield not subjected to concentrated fire was the small field at Haleiwa, where planes of the 47th Squadron, 15th Pursuit Group, were located. When the attack began on Wheeler Field, certain members of the 47th Squadron made their way to Haleiwa by automobile. Here, acting without any information as to the number or

21

type of enemy planes, six pilots took to the air in P-36's and P-40's, making two flights between 0815 and 1000. In the first flight were 1st Lt. John J. Webster, 2d Lts. John L. Dains, Kenneth M. Taylor, and George S. Welch in P-40's, and 1st Lt. Robert J. Rogers flying a P-36. In the second flight were Lieutenant Dains in a P-36 and Lieutenants Rogers, Taylor, Welch, and 2d Lt. Harry M. Brown in P-40's. These pilots accounted for a total of seven enemy aircraft. Four planes were shot down by Welch, two by Taylor, and one by Brown. Of the six pilots who took to the air from Haleiwa, only one lost his life in action on 7 December 1941. Lieutenant Dains, on his third flight that morning, was shot down over Schofield Barracks, probably by antiaircraft fire.

Not all of the Army planes which met the enemy over Oahu could engage in combat. Unarmed B-17's of the 38th and 88th Reconnaissance Squadrons, completing the first leg of a flight to the Philippines, arrived at Oahu in the midst of the attack. By means of skillful maneuvering the planes were landed at various points on the island. Lts. Frank P. Bostrom, Harry N. Brandon, Robert E. Thacker, David G. Rawls, and Harold N. Chaffin, led by Maj. Richard H. Carmichael, of the 88th Squadron, arrived at Oahu shortly after 0800. Lieutenant Bostrom was pursued by the enemy planes almost all the way around the island; after outflying them and with only a few minutes' supply of gasoline remaining, he brought the new B-17 down on a golf course. Lieutenants Brandon, Thacker, and Rawls flew through antiaircraft fire and enemy gun fire to execute successful landings at Hickam

Field, where crew members were strafed as they sought shelter in ditches. Major Carmichael and Lieutenant Chaffin, unable to land at Hickam or Wheeler because of fires on the ground, managed to bring their planes down safely at Haleiwa, though the effective length of the field was only 1,200 feet.

Maj. Truman H. Landon, commanding the flight of the 38th Reconnaissance Squadron, led his planes through to safe landings. One of the B-17's, piloted by Lt. Robert H. Richards, was subjected to an attack by several enemy aircraft, resulting in serious injury to two crew members and in damage to the plane. With ailerons damaged beyond use, a downwind landing was made on a short runway without further injury to crew members. While the B-17's were not able to provide any opposition in their first meeting with the enemy, they were soon armed and placed in use by the Hawaiian Air Force.

Throughout the remainder of 7 December, P-40's, A-20's, B-17's, B-18's, and O-47's searched for enemy surface craft in the waters surrounding Oahu. Between 0950 and 1520 a total of 37 sorties were made. The aircraft warning system had been put back into operation shortly after 0800, but it failed to furnish any reliable information on aircraft returning to the carriers. The Japanese force of three or four carriers and attendant craft, by maintaining radio silence, had not been detected in approaching Oahu from the north; with the same elusiveness the force slipped away from the island, unseen by American patrol and reconnaissance planes.

Aftermath

In comparison with the results achieved, Japanese losses were insignificant. Army forces accounted for 20 enemy aircraft, while naval forces took a toll of three submarines of 45 tons each and 28 aircraft. Other planes were probably forced down at sea before reaching their carriers. Nevertheless, these losses represented a small price to pay for crippling the Pacific Fleet, wiping out much of the air strength on Oahu, and destroying military and naval installations on the island. There could be no doubt of the immediate success of the attack, which was greatly aided by the elements of surprise and deception. If the total Japanese objective, however, was the annihilation of the Pacific Fleet, then the attack was only partially successful. The Fleet was temporarily disabled and immobilized, but not permanently lost. Within a few months 3 battleships, 3 cruisers, and 2 other craft which had been damaged were put back into active service. After extensive repair and salvage efforts, by the end of 1942 it was evident that of all the vessels sunk or damaged at Pearl Harbor, only one—the 26-year-old battleship _Arizona_—was a total loss.

Whatever extent of destruction the Japanese hoped to achieve in their attack on Pearl Harbor, they were not at that moment interested in seizing the Hawaiian Islands. Their primary objective lay in the islands off southeast Asia and in the western Pacific. After the lightning blow at Pearl Harbor the Japanese were assured of a considerable period of time in which they could proceed with their program of expansion unhampered by the Pacific Fleet.

The Japanese were careful to include in their plans the capture of American steppingstones to the Far East. The attack on Oahu was, therefore, only one of a series of widespread assaults throughout the Pacific. On 7 December the Midway Islands were subjected to 30 minutes of shelling by a force estimated at two cruisers and two destroyers, which approached from the south and opened fire at 2130 Midway time (2330 Honolulu time). Shortly before noon on 8 December (1450, 7 December, Honolulu time) approximately 27 land-based aircraft bombed and strafed Wake Island. Farther west, the island of Guam, surrounded by Japanese bases, fiercely resisted enemy assaults until 13 December. Sustained attacks on Wake finally resulted in its fall on 22 December after a gallant defense by Marine forces on the island. Other attacks on the Philippines, Malaya, and Hong Kong indicated the range of Japanese intentions and the wide scope of operations in which American and British forces in the Far East were suddenly engaged.

As had been expected by American military strategists, war with Japan also brought war with the members of the Rome-Berlin Axis. The task which the AAF was assigned in the global conflict was gigantic in proportions, and the losses suffered on 7 December offered no comfort to those who had been given the difficult assignment. On this one day approximately two-thirds of the combat planes in the Philippines and Hawaii were either destroyed or damaged. The total aircraft strength of the entire AAF was only 3,000 planes, and of these only 1,157 were suitable for combat action.

It had been envisaged that the United States might be drawn

into war with Japan and the Axis simultaneously, and plans for deployment of the AAF had been shaped accordingly. The power of the German military machine and the extent of German resources indicated that the first objective should be destruction of the industrial facilities which made it possible for Germany to wage war, the destruction to be accomplished by long-range bombers operating against specific targets with the highly developed technique of precision bombing. This pre-war plan further stipulated that while the major effort was being made in Europe, forces in the Pacific would have to maintain the "strategic defensive."

Although changes and revisions of certain estimates had to be made, this plan remained the basis for AAF action when war came. The forces then available were admittedly insufficient for carrying out either phase of the strategy, but the objectives were clear. The primary consideration of national defense required that the Axis be defeated first and that positions in the Pacific be held until the offensive could be launched against Japan. The AAF offensive against Germany, however, could not be undertaken even on a small scale until approximately 8 months after the outbreak of war, pending the training of a sufficient number of bombardment crews, the building of a large force of heavy bombers, and the preparation of adequate bases in Great Britain. During these months the air units in the Pacific and China-Burma-India theaters were in almost daily combat with a fanatical enemy whose offensive power seemed almost to have no limits.

III.

THE FAR EAST AIR FORCE IN THE PHILIPPINES

The Far East Air Force, situated astride the line of Japanese advance in the Western Pacific, became the first Army air force to participate in extended operations in World War II. Defenders of the Philippines were destined to fight a losing battle, but the action was nevertheless important--not only for its delaying effect on enemy plans but also for its revelation of tactical principles which contributed to later American successes in the war. Operating against overwhelming enemy forces, and with inadequate facilities, few supplies, and only small reinforcements, members of the Far East Air Force over a period of 5 months, extracted a toll from the enemy far out of proportion to their meager means.

On the first day of war General Brereton's command suffered the loss of almost half its aircraft. Within 3 days pursuit planes had to be withdrawn from active combat and conserved for reconnaissance purposes. Within 10 days after the outbreak of hostilities the powerful and rapid enemy advance forced all heavy bombers to fall back to the Netherlands East Indies, where the struggle was continued. But this phase of operations was likewise destined to be futile, and early in March the few remaining planes were forced back to Australia, where they provided a nucleus for the Fifth Air Force. The familiar pattern of "defeat and retreat" was not altered until Allied air forces in the Southwest Pacific could build up sufficient strength to offer effective opposition to the enemy's air power. In the Philippines, the dwindling number of pursuit planes continued in action until the end of formal resistance on 8 May, Air Corps personnel sharing the common fate of those who stood on Bataan and at Corregidor.

When war came, American forces in the Philippines were not caught unawares. Perhaps their only surprise was that the first attack occurred in Hawaii and not in the Western Pacific. Air Corps units, alerted almost a month earlier, had rushed to complete dispersal areas around the airfields and to dig slit trenches and take other protective measures. Pursuit planes were kept armed, and all aircraft were held in flying readiness.

Only a few days prior to the outbreak of war the 14th and 93d Squadrons of the 19th Bombardment Group were sent from Clark Field to Del Monte Field, where the 5th Air Base Group was stationed. Remaining at Clark Field were the 28th and 30th Squadrons and Headquarters of the 19th Bombardment Group and the 20th Squadron and the Headquarters and Headquarters Squadron of the 24th Pursuit Group. The 21st Pursuit Squadron, equipped with P-35's, was stationed at Del Carmen Field, south of Clark. The 20th Air Base Group, 2d Observation Squadron, and 17th and 34th Pursuit Squadrons were at Nichols Field. Headquarters for the Far East Air Force and its bomber, interceptor, and service commands, the 36th Air Base Group, Philippine Air Depot, and 27th Bombardment Group were located at Nielson Field. The 3d Pursuit Squadron was at Iba Field, on the west coast of Luzon.

Early on the morning of 8 December (7 December, Honolulu time),

The Philippine Islands

at approximately 0400, the radar at Iba picked up a large formation of aircraft over the China Sea headed towards Corregidor. The 3d Pursuit Squadron was sent to intercept the formation; but with no information available on the altitude of the approaching planes, the P-40's failed to effect an interception and returned to Iba for refueling. The reported formation apparently turned back to sea.

Official word of the attack on Pearl Harbor was sent to all units at 0430. An hour earlier the commercial radio at Clark Field had picked up news of the attack, and on the basis of this unverified information, units were ordered to stations. At Del Monte Field official word of hostilities in Hawaii was received at 0630. Two B-17's were then dispatched on reconnaissance missions around the coast of Mindanao, but nothing was found to indicate enemy movements. The island of Luzon, rather than Mindanao, was first on the Japanese plan of attack in the Philippines.

The enemy feint at 0400 was followed by another at 0930, when a large formation of aircraft was reported over Lingayen Gulf flying in the direction of Manila. When the air alarm sounded, at Clark Field, B-17's were put into the air to avoid being caught on the ground. The 17th Pursuit Squadron was ordered to cover Clark, while the 20th Squadron was sent north to intercept the approaching planes in the vicinity of Rosales. But the enemy formation, instead of proceeding south, swung sharply to the northeast and hit the military installations at Baguio and also airfields at Cabantuan, south of Baguio.

The Attack on Clark Field

By 1130 the P-40's of the 20th Pursuit Squadron and B-17's of the 28th and 30th Bombardment Squadrons—with the exception of one plane still on reconnaissance—had landed at Clark Field and the bombers were being refueled for a mission to Formosa. The 17th Pursuit Squadron had returned to Nichols for refueling.

The 3d Pursuit Squadron, still at Iba, put all its operational P-40's in the air when radar indicated aircraft approaching from over the China Sea. Realizing that the approaching aircraft might elude the 3d Squadron, interceptor headquarters dispatched the 17th Squadron from Nichols Field to cover Bataan Peninsula while the 34th Squadron was ordered to patrol over Manila. The 3d Squadron, after failing to intercept, headed back to Iba, as its gasoline supply was running low. The P-40's were circling the field when approximately 54 enemy bombers and a number of dive bombers attacked. Eight P-40's on the ground and the installations at Iba were destroyed. Fighters in the air shot down one bomber and drove off a number of aircraft which attempted to strafe the field after the bombing attack. Five P-40's were shot down and three crash-landed on the beach after running out of gasoline. The remainder of the squadron landed at O'Donnell Field to the east of Iba.

While this action was taking place, another formation of enemy planes was reported at approximately 1130 heading south over Lingayen Gulf. Because the P-40's and B-17's at Clark Field were still refueling, the P-35's of the 21st Pursuit Squadron at Del Carmen were ordered to cover Clark, but were considerably delayed in taking off by thick clouds of dust. By 1215 the pursuits at Clark were ready to take off to cover the field. Four of the P-40's had just taken to the air, 5 were in the process of taking off, and 5 more were on the ground when the field was attacked by approximately 75 enemy bombers. These were followed by a large number of dive bombers and fighters which swept in to strafe the field.

The sole fighter opposition to enemy planes was provided by the four P-40's which had just taken off. These planes of the 20th Squadron accounted for four Japanese aircraft, two of which were shot down by 2d Lt. Randall D. Keator. The P-35's of the 21st Squadron, delayed by dust at Del Carmen, did not arrive over Clark Field until the attack had ended. The 17th Squadron patrolling over Bataan and the 34th Squadron over Manila could not be summoned immediately because one of the first bombs dropped on Clark Field had destroyed the radio station. The 17th eventually arrived over Clark, but only after the attacking planes had withdrawn.

Throughout the 90-minute assault the men on the ground displayed the same disregard for their lives that had been demonstrated earlier at Hickam, Wheeler, and Bellows fields on Oahu. The number of casualties was high and the damage to aircraft and installations extensive. At least 55 officers and men were killed and 110 wounded. Of the 22 B-17's and 10 P-40's which did not get into the air, only seven B-17's escaped complete destruction and only two or three of these escaped damage. Most of the hangars and buildings around the field were destroyed.

The Japanese at the end of 9 December had succeeded in wiping out half the heavy-bomber force and one-third of the pursuit strength of the Far East Air Force. Of the combat aircraft only 17 B-17's, 15 P-35's, and 50 to 55 P-40's remained, many of them damaged. Repair and maintenance of these aircraft would be extremely difficult in view of the destruction of spare parts and depot facilities.

The First Week

During the night of 8 December the ground crews at Clark Field salvaged planes which had been partially destroyed and attempted to put other planes into flying condition. The remaining planes and personnel of the 3d Pursuit Squadron, which had been almost decimated at Iba, were divided between the 34th Squadron at Nichols Field and the 17th Squadron, which was to be transferred to Clark Field.

Before this transfer was effected, one flight of the 17th Squadron was dispatched to intercept a formation of enemy aircraft approaching the Manila area from the north early on the morning of 9 December. Dust on the field again hampered the take-off and resulted in the wrecking of two planes and the death of one pilot. The enemy formation, consisting of approximately 10 bombers, flew over Fort McKinley at a high altitude and dropped one bomb, then proceeded to unload the remaining bombs on Nichols Field at 0315. Three officers and enlisted men were killed and 15 wounded, one hanger was destroyed by fire, and two planes were damaged. The four P-40's which took to the air were unable to accomplish interception in the dark.

Except for this action, the second day of war in the Philippines was comparatively quiet for the air forces. The damage at Clark Field made it impossible for the bombers to carry out offensive operations.

Throughout the day, repair work was rushed while plans were shaped for a mission on 10 December. Only the B-17's based at Del Monte had escaped enemy fire, and these planes would have to stage through Luzon in order to strike at the enemy's advance from the north. Accordingly, late in the afternoon of 9 December eight B-17's from Del Monte were sent to San Marcelino, an uncompleted field near Bataan Peninsula, where they were fired on by ground troops but nevertheless succeeded in landing. Although six more B-17's completed the flight to Clark Field at 1430, they were forced to take off again immediately after landing and to remain aloft until after dark to escape a threatened air attack on the field.

By this time reports had been received of enemy convoys off Aparri and Vigan in northern Luzon, and on 10 December the Far East Air Force concentrated on vessels in these two areas. Five B-17's under the command of Maj. Cecil E. Combs took off from Clark Field at 0600 for an attack at Vigan, escorted by P-40's of the 17th Squadron. The 21st Squadron, with its P-35's, was slower in reaching the target. Loaded with 100-pound bombs, the B-17's made runs on enemy transports, hitting several of the vessels and possibly sinking one. Following the bombardment, the pursuit planes came down to a low altitude and made numerous strafing attacks. 1st Lt. Samuel H. Marrett led the 21st Squadron in setting two transports afire, and in a final attack on a third vessel he was killed when his plane was caught in the resulting explosion of the transport. One other pursuit plane was lost during the attacks.

After expending their ammunition the P-35's returned to Del Carmen, and the P-40's covered Clark Field while the B-17's landed. The bombers were being refueled when an air alarm was sounded; three of the five planes were ordered to take off. In the air they received radio orders to proceed to Del Monte, but because of a gasoline shortage two of the planes landed at San Jose, Mindoro, and one at Tacloban, Leyte.

From the 14th Squadron's B-17's at San Marcelino, five flew to Clark Field early in the morning to pick up bomb loads. The crews were instructed to search for an aircraft carrier reported near Aparri, and their planes were partially loaded with bombs when an air raid alarm at 0930 caused all aircraft to be ordered off the ground. Those planes with bombs proceeded to make individual attacks.

One of the bombers, piloted by Capt. Colin P. Kelly, Jr., flew over Aparri, where crew members counted 6 cruisers, 10 destroyers, 15 to 20 transports, and a large battleship offshore. After 30 minutes of unsuccessful searching for the aircraft carrier, Captain Kelly decided to attack the battleship, although only three 600-pound bombs had been loaded before take-off. Released in train, the bombs scored one direct hit and two near misses, leaving the battleship smoking and trailing oil. As the B-17 neared Clark Field it was attacked by enemy pursuit planes. The left rear gunner was killed, and the plane was set afire. When flames spread through the radio compartment and smoke began pouring into the pilot's compartment, Captain Kelly ordered the crew to bail out. All except the pilot and co-pilot had made the jump when the plane exploded. The co-pilot was thrown clear and parachuted to safety, but Captain Kelly's parachute did not open.

The employment of heavy bombers on 10 December was not entirely in accordance with prescribed practice, but not because the crews and operations officers were lacking in training. Inadequate communications with outlying fields, insufficient protection of airfields, and the consequent necessity of putting planes into the air for their protection added to the difficulty of operations. All these conditions, together with the extremely limited number of planes available, made it impossible to operate according to the standard procedure of pattern bombing. Rarely did B-17's at Clark Field have time for refueling and bomb-loading before another air raid alarm would put them into the air. Indeed, with the ground echelon of Japanese air units moving into Aparri on 10 December it was clear that bombers could no longer operate from Luzon, for enemy air superiority would be overwhelming.

Events of 10 December not only affected future operation of the B-17's, but likewise changed the use of remaining pursuit planes. After protective cover and strafing missions of the morning, all available pursuit aircraft—now concentrated in the 17th, 21st, and 34th Squadrons—had been put into the air to intercept a large number of enemy planes approaching the Manila area from the north. The formation of approximately 27 high-altitude bombers was protected by a large force of fighter planes, exceeding the Far East Air Force intercepting planes by about 100. With the exception of 1st Lts. Joseph H. Moore and William A. Sheppard, the pursuit pilots were unable to break through the tight cover and reach the enemy bombers. The action for the most part was confined to dog-fights over Manila Bay.

The enemy bombers concentrated on Nichols Field and the naval base at Cavite, south of Manila. Huge fires at Cavite completely destroyed the naval supply depot and industrial facilities, including the power plant. One submarine was a total loss, while another submarine and two destroyers were slightly damaged. No further demonstrations of enemy air superiority were needed to convince naval officials that units of the Asiatic Fleet were not safe in Manila Bay. That night two destroyers, two submarine tenders, and five small auxiliary vessels sailed for friendly ports to the south of the Philippines. Patrol Wing Ten, with its Catalinas, continued to operate against enemy vessels until 14 December, when with less than one squadron in operating condition the wing was moved to the Netherlands East Indies. From the wrecked and damaged planes left behind, officers and men assembled four complete planes. Two of these later evacuated high-ranking Army and Navy officers from the Philippines, while the other two stayed in the fight until they were demolished.

The depletion of air forces in the Philippines by the close of 10 December called for a decision as to the deployment of remaining aircraft. The number of pursuit planes had been reduced to 22 P-40's and 8 P-35's, and all observation planes had been destroyed or seriously damaged by enemy air attacks. The continued use of pursuit planes to intercept superior forces would in all probability result in wiping out the few P-40's and P-35's within a few days. With enemy units moving into northern Luzon, General MacArthur's ground forces would need information which could be gained only by aerial reconnaissance.

The decision was therefore made to use the pursuit planes mainly for observation; no further attempts would be made to meet enemy forces in the air. On many of their missions, however, the planes bombed and strafed targets of opportunity and occasionally were sent on attack missions against enemy landing forces and airfields.

While enemy forces were pouring into Aparri and Vigan, two more convoys moved up to the coasts of Luzon, one at Zambales on the west and one at Legaspi on the southeast. Pursuit planes on 11 December gathered information as to the composition of these forces and at the same time strafed enemy seaplanes and vessels. Six of the remaining B-17's of the 19th Bombardment Group, now at Del Monte, attempted to join in the assault on forces at Legaspi on 14 December, after making two sorties against enemy shipping at Vigan on 12 December. Of the six planes which started on the mission to Legaspi, one failed to get into the air because of a blown-out tire, and two were forced to turn back by engine trouble. One of the remaining planes was attacked by six enemy fighters after bombs had been dropped on transports. With two engines dead the plane made a crash-landing at Masbate. All crew members were saved, but the plane was later destroyed by enemy strafing.

Another B-17, piloted by 1st Lt. Hewitt T. Wheless, was attacked by 18 enemy planes as it approached the target. For 25 minutes the enemy aircraft continued to attack the B-17 as it flew back toward Del Monte. All four gunners were wounded, one fatally. Some enemy pilots, after emptying their ammunition into the B-17's, flew alongside the big plane and peered into the pilot's compartment, evidently amazed that the bomber could still fly. The plane was completely riddled, one engine and the radio were shot out, the oxygen system was destroyed, the rear wheel was shot off, the front wheels were punctured, and seven out of 11 control cables were shot away, but Lieutenant Wheless made a successful crash-landing on a small field at Cagayen, Mindanao.

Withdrawal of B-17's to Australia

In the first week of war the B-17's had demonstrated their durability; in combat action they were proving to be real "Flying Fortresses," but the continued basing of B-17's in the Philippines was hardly possible. Del Monte—the only field on Mindanao suitable for heavy bombers—had no protecting aircraft or repair facilities and only limited supplies of bombs and ammunition. Clearly, the field could be used only as an advanced base. For a more permanent base the B-17's were forced to fall back 1,500 miles southward, to Batchelor Field, near Darwin, Australia. Between 17 and 20 December the B-17's, now reduced to a total of 14, flew to the new station. From there some of them had to fly a similar distance to Laverton, near Melbourne, for depot overhaul.

While Batchelor Field offered comparative safety from enemy attack, its location was not entirely suitable for the intended operations. The plan was to operate from Australia against targets in the Philippines, but the distance proved to be too great for effective results. Accordingly, the bombers remained at Batchelor only long enough to carry out two missions. On 22 December, nine of the planes, each loaded with four 500-pound bombs, flew into the southern

Philippines and hit ships concentrated at Davao, where enemy landings had begun 2 days earlier. Because of a light overcast, results could not be determined. Despite the distances involved in this mission, these nine B-17's represented the largest formation to be put over a target during the month of December. They landed at Del Monte for refueling and another load of bombs. Before dawn the next morning four of the planes took off for Lingayen Gulf, where they attacked enemy shipping. The remaining planes, unable to effect a rendezvous, returned to Batchelor Field.

The second mission from Australia occurred on 24 December when three B-17's flew to Del Monte, where they were to receive further orders. Unable to find any orders and likewise unsuccessful in contacting Manila, two of the planes on the next day bombed the Davao airfield, while the third plane remained at Del Monte because of a damaged tire. 1st Lts. George E. Scheetzel and Alvin J. Mueller, pilots of the two attacking planes, maneuvered the craft through heavy pursuit fire both before and after the bombs were dropped on the enemy-held airfield. The two B-17's limped back to Batchelor Field, and the third plane returned after bombing shipping at Davao. This last bombing mission of December was followed by several days of repair and overhaul work, when the B-17's were readied for flights to Malang, Java, their next base.

Fighter Operations

In the meantime, pursuit squadrons in the Philippines, under orders to avoid direct combat, were performing reconnaissance missions over

Luzon and harassing enemy holdings around the coast. On 13 December the commander of the 17th Pursuit Squadron, Lt. Boyd D. Wagner, while on a reconnaissance mission to Aparri, shot down four enemy pursuit planes and then destroyed a number of planes on the ground by strafing. Three days later Lieutenant Wagner led a flight of three planes against the airfield at Vigan, where supply dumps and 17 enemy planes were strafed and hit with 30-pound fragmentation bombs. The attack was carried out in the face of heavy antiaircraft fire. The plane piloted by 1st Lt. Russell M. Church was hit and set afire before bombs were released. Rather than bail out, Lieutenant Church went into a dive, released his bombs, and then crashed.

When the Japanese began landing operations at San Miguel Bay in southern Luzon on 23 December, all available planes of the 24th Pursuit Group were loaded with 30-pound fragmentation bombs and sent to oppose the landing. Out of 12 P-40's and 6 P-35's in the attack, 2 P-35's were damaged by antiaircraft fire to such an extent that crash landings were necessary. It was not expected that the pursuit planes would be able to halt the enemy landings, but they did provide a measure of opposition.

The absence of American naval forces in the waters surrounding the Philippines gave the Japanese complete freedom of movement and allowed them to place their forces at any point at will. After 2 weeks of war they had landed sizable forces on the island of Luzon and were operating pursuit aircraft from fields at Aparri, Vigan, and Legaspi. From this time forward, enemy air attacks on the defenders of Luzon were frequent and heavy. In the ground fighting the major enemy effort appeared to be along the Aringay-Agoo-San Fabian line, where from 80,000 to 100,000 Japanese were being concentrated. To meet these forces General MacArthur had approximately 40,000 men in partially equipped units. The disparity in size between the opposing forces determined the course for the defenders. Except for outright surrender to the numerically superior forces, the only logical course was to fight a delaying action on successive lines in central Luzon. General MacArthur determined upon such a plan, which foresaw a final defensive position in Bataan, north of the fortress island of Corregidor.

For years Corregidor had been envisaged as "the final citadel of American resistance in the Philippine Islands." As the largest of four islands commanding the entrance to Manila Bay, it was strongly fortified by huge guns embedded in the rocky surface. Fort Mills, the Army post on the island, had barracks on top of the rock, but numerous underground installations--including a hospital, bomb shelters, and tunnels equipped with trolley cars--made up the elaborate defenses. There was also one small landing field, Kindley Field. Three smaller forts supplemented Corregidor's guns: Fort Hughes on Caballo Island, Fort Drum on Fraile Island, and Fort Frank on Carabao Island.

So long as General MacArthur's forces could hold Corregidor and other Manila Bay defenses, the harbor and naval base would be useless to the Japanese, whose capture of Manila seemed inevitable. In order to spare the civilian population General MacArthur on 24 December arranged for the removal of the Philippine government from Manila to

Corregidor, withdrew his forces toward Bataan, and then declared Manila an open city. The Japanese, disregarding the proclamation, continued to subject the defenseless city to merciless bombing attacks until its occupation on 2 January.

Bataan

The tactical situation determined the employment of the Far East Air Force during the remainder of the Philippine campaign. Because of overwhelming enemy air superiority and lack of suitable bases, the heavy bombers had already been sent to Australia. The withdrawal of Army forces to Bataan meant that the few remaining pursuit planes had to move to bases on the peninsula, a step accompanied by the move of Far East Air Force headquarters to Australia. On Christmas Eve, when General MacArthur's forces were withdrawn from Manila, General Brereton and a skeleton staff of officers left Luzon in two Catalinas for the south. Their mission was to establish the necessary bases and facilities for operations from Australia through Mindanao against the enemy on Luzon. One of the planes flew directly to Darwin, where Lt. Col. Charles H. Caldwell, the senior officer, set up temporary headquarters at a field used by the Royal Australian Air Force. General Brereton, having been authorized to cooperate with forces of the Netherlands East Indies, as well as with Australian forces, stopped at Soerabaja and Batavia long enough to make preliminary arrangements for the use of air bases in that area.

Upon arriving at Darwin on 29 December, General Brereton continued negotiations for the use of certain facilities in Australia. Prior to the outbreak of war General MacArthur had been given the responsibility for developing the eastern end of the South Pacific ferry route, along with establishing a ferry route for pursuit aircraft from Australia to the Philippines via Koepang, Kendari, Sandakan, Balikpapan, Tarakan, Del Monte, and Santa Barbara (on Panay). As commander of the Far East Air Force, General Brereton had held conferences with Australian and NEI officials regarding the project. Plans for staff coordination and for the use of Australian facilities were formulated and were being put into action when the war began. This groundwork proved to be useful when the course of events forced the Far East Air Force to seek bases outside the Philippines.

Air Force units remaining in the Philippines were placed under the command of Col. Harold H. George of the V Interceptor Command. Throughout the epic defense of Bataan the pursuit aircraft served as all-purpose planes. They bombed enemy landings on Bataan, strafed and bombed enemy aircraft at Nichols and Nielson Fields, attacked shipping in Subic Bay, and intercepted numerous air attacks on Corregidor; they photographed enemy artillery positions at Cavite, performed reconnaissance missions as far north as Lingayen, ferried medical supplies from Mindanao to Bataan, and transported personnel from Bataan and Corregidor to Mindanao. In short, the dwindling number of aircraft operated by the 24th Pursuit Group had to function as an entire air force.

Comparatively few Air Corps officers and men in the Philippines had an opportunity to perform the duties for which they had been trained. Except for a handful of pilots and maintenance men, the bulk of air personnel in Luzon were used as infantry and shared the fate of the other defenders of Bataan.

Efforts to Reinforce the Philippines

While withdrawing to Bataan, American leaders made provisions for continuing the fight from other islands of the Philippines, and extensive preparations were undertaken in anticipation of air reinforcement from the United States. Brig. Gen. William F. Sharp, commanding the Mindanao-Visayan forces, was instructed to continue to resist the enemy by using guerrilla tactics. General Sharp had at his disposal three divisions of Philippine Army troops, comprising approximately 30,000 officers and men, and more than 500 American officers and men in addition to about 1,200 Air Corps personnel of the 5th Air Base Group and attached units.

Maj. Ray T. Elsmore, commanding the group, had arrived at Del Monte a week prior to the beginning of war when preparations were under way for the construction of barracks and other facilities at the field. The beginning of hostilities and the landing of Japanese troops at Davao did not seriously interfere with the activities of Air Corps units on Mindanao. While the forces underwent infantry training and many of the personnel were placed in command of infantry units, the bulk of the air force troops worked day and night to build additional airfields and dispersal areas. On 1 January approximately 650 members of the 19th Bombardment Group were added to the infantry forces on Mindanao. Three nights before, they had boarded a small inter-island steamer at Mariveles, and after slipping through minefields and undergoing an attack by a Japanese flying boat, they arrived safely at Mindanao.

Maintaining Del Monte as an operational base for all types of aircraft was one of the chief responsibilities of Major Elsmore, who became air officer on General Sharp's staff. Careful camouflage and dispersal procedures gave a maximum amount of protection to planes which landed at the field long enough to refuel and take off again for attacks in the Philippines. Aircraft which had to remain on the field during daylight were painstakingly covered with enormous quantities of coconut leaves, 10 truckloads of leaves being required to cover one B-17. The existence of Del Monte made possible the evacuation of many officers and men who otherwise would not have escaped the fate of the Philippines.

More remarkable perhaps than the maintaining of Del Monte until the fall of the Philippines was the extensive construction program carried out on Mindanao by air base forces working in the very shadow of the Japanese at Davao. Plans included the building of airfields on Mindanao and other islands in preparation for driving the Japanese out of the northern Philippines. Air base personnel were accordingly scattered throughout Mindanao to select suitable sites and to procure native labor for the projects. Within a short time auxiliary fields had been constructed at Malabang, Maramag, Valencia, and Anakin, and a seaplane base was prepared at Lake Lanao. By the first of April 1942 there were 21 airfields on Mindanao suitable for heavy bombers and also a number of smaller landing strips, all well-concealed and hidden from the enemy.

Even though heavy bombers were, for the time being, forced to seek bases outside the Philippines, the situation was by no means regarded as hopeless; and more B-17's were started on their way from the United States. The Pacific ferry route via Midway and Wake could not be used after the opening of hostilities, and the new route via the South Pacific was still incomplete.*/ But until the fall of Java it was possible to send heavy-bomber replacements for the Far East by way of the South Atlantic, Africa, India, Sumatra, and Java.

Japanese penetration in the Netherlands East Indies, however, prevented the bombers from being used against the enemy in the Philippines. The encirclement of the Philippines, moreover, meant that pursuit planes and dive bombers could not be brought in by boat. The need for erection facilities, as well as a supply base to the rear of the actual fighting, had resulted in an early decision to center such activities in Australia, but here again all efforts met with disappointment. The first air reinforcements to arrive in Australia were in a convoy en route to the Philippines when hostilities began. Consisting of eight transports and freighters, escorted by the cruiser Pensacola, the convoy carried 2,600 Air Corps troops (including 48 pilots) and 2,000 other troops (including two regiments of field artillery), as well as the usual troop equipment and approximately 340 motor vehicles, forty-eight 75-mm. guns, and large supplies of ammunition, bombs, and aviation fuel. Aircraft aboard

---
*/ The first B-17 to reach Australia via the South Pacific route arrived early in January.

included 18 P-40's and 52 unassembled A-24's destined for the 27th Bombardment Group already in the Philippines. Among the air force personnel on board the transport Republic were the ground echelons of headquarters squadron, the 11th and 22d Squadrons of the 7th Bombardment Group, the 8th Materiel Squadron, and the 88th Reconnaissance Squadron, whose air echelon flew into Oahu on 7 December.

After leaving Hawaii on 29 November the convoy took a southwestward course instead of the normal course through the Japanese-mandated islands. The vessels had crossed the equator when word was received on 7 December that hostilities had begun. Protective measures were taken and as many guns as could be found were set up on improvised mounts, but five of the boats were entirely without armament. Even after picking up more guns at Suva in the Fiji Islands, the convoy was still not adequately prepared to ward off any attack. An attempt could still be made to get the vessels to the Philippines, but by 12 December the possibility of safe arrival was so slight that the convoy was ordered to Australia. Brig. Gen. Julian F. Barnes, troop commander of the Republic, was ordered to assume command of all U. S. troops in Australia, to report to General MacArthur for further instructions, and to erect aircraft in the cargo for ferrying to the Philippines.

Preparations were under way in Australia for receiving the convoy and forwarding aerial reinforcements to the Philippines as quickly as possible. The U. S. military attaché in Australia, Col. Van S. Merle-Smith, acting under instructions from Washington, was making tentative arrangements for erection of aircraft and disposition of the vessels. In addition, Brig. Gen. Henry B. Clagett was sent by air from Luzon on 18 December to organize the Air Corps units expected at Brisbane. In the opinion of General MacArthur the convoy might still be sent to the Philippines if sufficient naval escort were provided. Accordingly, he planned for the Air Corps units to be left at Brisbane for erecting aircraft, while the remaining troops and materiel were to be moved on to the Philippines if General Barnes considered the voyage possible.

On 21 December, when General Barnes received these instructions from General MacArthur, he was notified by the War Department that Maj. Gen. George H. Brett, who was en route from conferences in the Middle East and China, had been named commander of U. S. forces in Australia. The new commander was assigned the mission of setting up a supply system and of getting supplies to the forces in the Philippines. En route to his new post General Brett held conferences with British officials in India and with Dutch authorities in Java, delaying his arrival in Australia until the first of January.

During the last week of December there was considerable activity around Brisbane as hurried preparations were made to dispose of the convoy in accordance with General MacArthur's desires. Pending the arrival of General Brett, General Clagett assumed command when he reached Brisbane on 22 December. On the following day the convoy debarked, and troops were quartered on the grounds of Ascot and Doomben race tracks, with tenting and messing facilities provided by the

Australian Army. Arrangements had been made for the use of Archerfield and Amberley airdromes by American troops for erection of aircraft in the convoy.

Several factors hampered the rapid execution of plans. The convoy had been loaded on a peacetime basis, with no effort made to place equipment on the same vessel with its designated unit. As a result, the entire cargo had to be unloaded, sorted, and reloaded before any vessels could be sent north to the Philippines. Even with dock laborers working 24 hours a day, this cumbersome process took 6 days for completion. By 28 December the vessels in the convoy were able to start on their way to the Philippines, but 4 days later their destination was changed to Darwin because of the rapidly deteriorating situation. The 48 pilots who had debarked at Brisbane—some of them still aviation cadets—needed additional training before they could be allowed to take aircraft into combat, and the planes had to be assembled before any training could be given.

In order to get the A-24's and P-40's into the Philippines as quickly as possible, a number of pilots were sent to Australia by plane. Before dawn on 18 December, 20 pilots of the 27th Bombardment Group and their commander, Maj. John H. Davies, climbed into two old B-18's and a C-39 and left Luzon on what they thought would be a 10-day mission for their A-24's. These flyers were followed on 1 January by a limited number of experienced pursuit pilots from the Philippines.

A variety of circumstances combined to prevent any of these pilots from returning to the Philippines with the planes which had arrived in the convoy. The assembling of the planes was accomplished in short order; but insofar as combat usefulness was concerned, the aircraft might just as well have been left in their crates. There was no Prestone for the P-40's, while the A-24's were minus trigger motors, solenoids, and gun mounts. A thorough search of the cargo disclosed no trace of the missing equipment. This situation only added to the disappointment of the 27th Group pilots, who had been caught without aircraft in the Philippines and who now had little hope of getting any of their planes into the Islands.

A sufficient amount of Prestone was eventually rounded up in Australia for the 18 P-40's, but the A-24 parts were not available locally. They were started on their way from the United States by air early in January. While waiting for the planes to be put in combat condition, the pursuit and dive-bomber pilots, under the direction of Maj. John H. Davies, carried out a training program and began to organize provisional squadrons. These efforts were of no direct benefit to the forces in the Philippines, for by the time the aircraft were ready for combat the opportunity for flying them to the Philippines had passed. Japanese landings at Tarakan Island (off northeast Borneo) and on the northern part of Celebes Island on 10 January cut into the pursuit ferry route from Australia and likewise endangered an alternate route which was under consideration. Less than 2 weeks later another stop on the original route was knocked out by enemy occupation of Balikpapan, in southeast Borneo.

Because of the rapid enemy advance and because of the difficulties in preparing planes and pilots for combat, no aerial reinforcements were flown into the Philippines after hostilities began. General MacArthur's forces were virtually cut off from the outside world. Occasional flights were made by heavy bombers from Australia to Del Monte, but the planes could stay on the field only long enough to unload their cargo of medical supplies and ammunition needed in Bataan. On return trips to Australia the bombers were taxed beyond their capacity in evacuating men from Mindanao. Water shipment of supplies was likewise a hazardous undertaking. Of seven ships sent from Australia only three arrived at Cebu, and then their cargo could not be transshipped to Bataan because of enemy interference.

As the Japanese net around the Philippines tightened with the passing weeks, blockade-running became almost futile; but in March one vessel from Australia bearing three crated P-40's succeeded in reaching Mindanao, where the planes were assembled and immediately put into action. With the exception of these three aircraft, no additional planes reached the Far East Air Force units in the Philippines. Though some of the pursuit, observation, and miscellaneous outmoded planes left in the Islands continued in action until the very end, the center of aerial operations after 8 weeks of war had shifted from the Philippines to the Netherlands East Indies.

-IV-

DEFENSE OF THE NETHERLANDS EAST INDIES

Conquest of the Philippines was not the ultimate objective of the Japanese; it was only one phase of a program of aggression in widespread areas throughout the Far East and the Pacific. While vast numbers of enemy troops were pouring into the Philippines during December, others were pounding the British garrison at Hong Kong, filtering through Thailand, and landing on Borneo. Hong Kong capitulated on 25 December under concentrated land and air attacks. Japanese penetration of Thailand met with only token resistance, and a pact signed between the two governments on 11 December paved the way for further penetration into Malaya. The landings on the northern coast of Borneo on 11 December, while constituting a part of the encircling movement around the Philippines, likewise marked the initial encroachment in the Netherlands East Indies.

With its thousands of islands providing convenient steppingstones from the southeastern tip of Asia to Australia, the Netherlands East Indies occupied a strategic position of primary significance. More important, the archipelago was unusually rich in natural resources; large oil wells and abundant supplies of rubber, tin, spices, sugar, and other tropical products would add much to the resources available to the Japanese, while their loss would be a serious blow to Allied economy. For these reasons defense of the Netherlands East Indies against Japanese aggression assumed a major importance and evoked the maximum efforts of the American, British, Dutch, and Australian forces in that area.

Defensive preparations made by the Dutch prior to the war included the development of small but efficient air and naval forces. Approximately 200 planes of all types, largely of American make, comprised the air force. Approximately 4 cruisers, 6 destroyers, and 18 submarines, and a large number of small craft made up the naval forces. Army forces, numbering about 100,000 were composed mostly of native, or Indonesian troops incompletely equipped. The war had been under way only 1 week before the Dutch sent all the bombers in their air force to bases in Sumatra, where they were to aid the British in the defense of Malaya. This move left Borneo without aerial striking power, but for the moment the situation seemed to be more serious in Malaya than in Borneo. By 1 January the strength of the Dutch air force had been reduced to 158 planes of all types. These aircraft, even when combined with British and Australian air units in the area, were insufficient against numerically superior forces.

A similar disparity existed between the opposing naval forces. The British Far Eastern Fleet had been practically eliminated from the opening phase of the war when Japanese bombers on 10 December sank the new battleship *Prince of Wales* and the older battle cruiser *Repulse* just off Malaya. Only weak cruiser forces were then left to oppose the Japanese naval units. Attacks on Cavite naval base and Manila harbor had forced the U. S. Asiatic Fleet, with the exception of a few small vessels, to abandon the Philippine Islands. Patrol Wing Ten, with less than one complete squadron of Catalinas remaining, had to leave the

Philippines on 14 December for bases in the Netherlands East Indies. Vessels of the Asiatic Fleet sought shelter farther south at Darwin, where facilities were not entirely adequate but where repairs could be made with a relative degree of safety from enemy attack. An operational command was set up at Soerabaja, on the northeastern coast of Java, in order to coordinate fleet activities with those of the British and Dutch. The chief task of these latter two forces at the moment was in convoying troops to Singapore and protecting merchant shipping.

Their concentration on the tense situation in Malaya pointed up the need for aerial striking power in the eastern and northern part of the archipelago. The Japanese were pouring into Kuching, in the northern part of Borneo, after their landing on 16 December; and according to their usual plan of action, only a short time would elapse before their air forces would be operating from the island. In order to forestall this development and a similar development in the Davao region of Mindanao, General Brereton while en route to Australia in the latter part of December had conferred with officials in Java and made preliminary arrangements for basing the B-17's of the Far East Air Force in the Netherlands East Indies. Although the bombers had been sent to Darwin and original plans called for the establishment of Far East Air Force headquarters there, the difficulty of carrying out operations over great distances had indicated the need of bases farther north. General Brereton arrived at Darwin on 29 December, and by 1 January a total of 11 B-17's had made the flight from Darwin to Malang, about 60 miles inland from Soerabaja, Java. While Malang was to be the main base, operational plans called for the use of advanced airdromes on Borneo and Celebes.

Stopping at Samarinda, Borneo, long enough to refuel and take on bomb loads, 8 of the B-17's on 4 January flew to the Davao area where they dropped nearly 10 tons of bombs on enemy shipping. In this first successful mission from NEI bases, the B-17's were reported to have sunk 1 destroyer and scored 3 hits on a battleship. A second attack on Davao shipping made by 9 B-17's on 9 January, was not so successful. Four planes were forced to return without dropping their bombs, and poor visibility over the target hampered the remaining planes. An advanced airdrome at Kendari on Celebes was used for this attack.

More frequent operations could not be carried out because of the time-consuming process of flying from Malang to the advanced airdrome for refueling and bomb-loading, thence to the target, back to the advanced airdrome, and finally to Malang--the entire process requiring 3 days. Additional time was required for maintenance and repairs and the small number of available bombers limited the extent of damage to the enemy. However, prospects for the development of a larger striking force were considered good, for the air echelon of the 7th Bombardment Group was on its way from the United States, via Africa and India, in LB-30's and in new B-17E's with tail guns, improved waist guns, and power-operated turrets. Promise of at least a semblance of a balanced air force was held out by the A-24's and P-40's in Australia which were originally destined for the Philippines. If their assembly and the training of their pilots and crews could be completed in time, these

planes would add substantially to the effectiveness of the forces in Java.

Plans for the use of Australian facilities were unchanged by the shift of aerial operations to the Netherlands East Indies. Australia was still to be developed as a major supply base and reception center for reinforcements arriving from the United States. Maj. Gen. George H. Brett, who had been made commander of the U. S. forces in Australia, upon arrival at his new post on 1 January immediately made a survey of the situation. He first named Brig. Gen. Julian F. Barnes as his chief of staff and placed Brig. Gen. Henry B. Clagett in charge of the port at Townsville. Plans called for development of a large advance base in the Darwin area, where proximity to the Netherlands East Indies would facilitate the support of those operations. In addition to being the jumping-off point for tactical air units, Darwin would serve as a secondary base for first and second echelon maintenance. The Townsville area, on the northeast coast, was to be developed as a major repair, maintenance, and supply base; and the Brisbane area, farther south, as a larger maintenance and erection base and transshipment point for Townsville and Darwin. The reception and distribution center for troops arriving from the United States and also the headquarters for U. S. Army Forces in Australia were to be located at Melbourne, in order to effect better coördination with the RAAF and Australian Army officials. Before he had time to make more than preliminary arrangements, however, General Brett was ordered to Java in another command position.

The ABDA Command

The problem of coordinating operations in the Netherlands East Indies was enlarged with the arrival of American air and naval units in the islands. American, British, Dutch, and Australian forces were now fighting a common enemy throughout the vast area from the Malay Peninsula to New Guinea, but there was no unity of command and very little coordination of effort. To cope with this situation the United Nations announced on 2 January the formation of the American, British, Dutch, Australian Command (ABDA Command), to be under the British Gen. Sir Archibald P. Wavell. General Brett was made Deputy Supreme Commander, and General Brereton was named Deputy Chief of the Air Staff. Adm. Thomas C. Hart was placed in operational command of the combined naval forces, while the remaining staff positions were filled by other representatives of the member nations. Temporary command of the Far East Air Force was assumed by Col. Francis M. Brady; Col. Eugene L. Eubank continued to head the V Bomber Command, and General Barnes became commander of the U. S. Army Forces in Australia, which were still to support operations in the Netherlands East Indies.

Establishment of the ABDA Command did not actually get under way until the middle of January. General Wavell arrived on 10 January and formally took over the command 5 days later. On the 18th of the month headquarters was established at a remote mountain resort at Lembang, 10 miles north of Bandoeng, Java. Since communication facilities were not entirely satisfactory, some time had to be spent in improving them and also in equipping the headquarters. At the same time, the

Far East Air Force was moving its headquarters nearer the scene of operations, after having remained at Darwin until 14 January. Within 4 days, air force headquarters made three moves: first to Soerabaja, then to Batavia (headquarters for Dutch naval forces), and finally to Bandoeng on 18 January.

The B-17's of the 19th Bombardment Group were still based at Malang, and by 11 January they had been provided with new targets. Japanese landings on the small island of Tarakan, off northeast Borneo, and at Menado, on the northeastern top of Celebes, constituted a direct threat to the safety of advanced airdromes which had been used by the B-17's in their two attacks on the Philippines. From this time forward, with the exception of a flight to Del Monte on January 19, at which time Jolo in the Philippines was attacked, the bombers were used in an effort to stop the Japanese advance in the Netherlands East Indies. By using an advanced airdrome at Palembang, Sumatra, the planes were able to attack the enemy as far west as Sungei Patani, on the Malay Peninsula. In these widespread operations rarely could more than seven or eight planes be sent on a mission, even after the arrival of the air echelon of the 7th Bombardment Group.

The first LB-30's of the 7th Group arrived at Malang on 11 January, having flown from the United States via the South Atlantic route. Three days later the first B-17's to fly over the new South Pacific ferry route arrived in Java. Since facilities were still not complete along the Pacific route, most of the remaining bombers came by way of the Atlantic, and were based in Java at Malang, Djogjakarta, or Madioen. Though lacking in combat experience, the crews of the 7th

Group were put into action as soon as their planes could be made ready. Their first mission, on 16 and 17 January, gave the new crews a taste of what they could expect in operating against the Japanese; it likewise gave the Japanese a taste of the new B-17E.

Early on the morning of 16 January 3 LB-30's and 2 B-17E's flew from Malang to Kendari, where they were refueled and loaded with bombs. The LB-30's then attacked the airdrome at Langoan, 20 miles south of Menado, hitting the runway and parking areas. The bombers were intercepted by 5 Zeros, 1 of which was shot down. Only 1 of the LB-30's reached Malang; the other 2 made forced landings and were later rescued. The 2 B-17's, piloted by Maj. Conrad F. Necrason and Lt. J. L. Dufrane, bombed enemy transports in Menado Bay. After completion of the second bombing run, the planes were subjected to heavy fire from 15 enemy fighters, including 2 Messerschmitts. In accordance with their usual tactics the enemy planes pulled up from the rear and attacked what they thought was the most vulnerable part of the bombers. Five Zeros and 1 Messerschmitt were promptly shot down.

During the 40-minute battle Pvt. Arvid B. Hegdahl, tail-gunner on the plane piloted by Major Necrason, was wounded in the leg after he had shot down 2 fighters. At one of the side guns was M/Sgt. Louis T. Silva, 47-year old line chief of the 9th Bombardment Squadron. Because of the scarcity of experienced gunners, this veteran had insisted on accompanying his squadron commander on the first mission. Officially credited with downing 3 enemy aircraft, he also found time to assist in carrying the wounded tail-gunner to the forward part of the plane.*

After fighting off 15 enemy fighters the 2 B-17's landed at Kendari for refueling and medical aid. The plane piloted by Lieutenant Dufrane had one engine out of commission, while the other B-17 had only a few bullet holes in it. The bombers had already engaged in more than their share of action in their first combat, but they had little respite from enemy fire. At 0215 an air-raid alarm sounded at Kendari, and 5 enemy fighters were over the field instantly. Major Necrason took off in the face of the attacking planes. Servicing had not been completed on the other plane; it was destroyed on the ground. Major Necrason's crew fought off 3 enemy fighters and finally made a safe landing at Malang 6 hours later.

The use of Kendari and Samarinda as forward bases for heavy bombers was soon cut short by further Japanese advances. Possession of the valuable Balikpapan oil fields, just south of Samarinda, was one of the objectives of the enemy, but the fields were destroyed by the Dutch just prior to Japanese landings on 23 January. Simultaneous landings were made at Kendari, followed by others on Ambon Island, east of Kendari, on 30 January. Between 22 January and 2 February, while enemy convoys were moving through Macassar Strait, the American and Dutch air and naval forces attacked with all the strength they could muster. After this series of engagements the combined forces announced that 15 Japanese transports had been sunk and 22 damaged. In spite of the opposition, the Japanese succeeded in their landing attempts on

*/Five months later Sergeant Silva was killed in an airplane accident in Australia.

Borneo and Celebes. The fact that Japanese air forces were now within bombing range of Java meant that airfields on the island were no longer safe from enemy attack.

Pursuits and Dive Bombers

The first Japanese bombers were not long in putting in their appearance over Java, for on 3 February heavy attacks were made on Malang, Madioen, and Soerabaja. The airdrome at Madioen was severely damaged; and 31 Allied aircraft, including 4 B-17's, were destroyed. In these attacks the Japanese met opposition from American pursuit planes for the first time in the NEI campaign. The 17th Pursuit Squadron (Provisional) had been formed on 14 January from the pilots and P-40's available in Australia. The squadron had proceeded in two flights from Brisbane via Darwin, Koepang, and Waingapoo to Soerabaja, completing the flights on 24 and 25 January. During the enemy attack on Soerabaja, a flight of P-40's provided interception. One P-40 was lost, while enemy losses included 1 fighter and 1 bomber.

The number of P-40's flown from Australia to Java was not sufficient to provide interception for every enemy attack on the island. The inadequate warning system frequently did not give sufficient advance-notice for getting the planes into the air. It was only by operating from a well-hidden field ten miles southwest of Djombang that the pursuit planes were spared destruction on the ground. More P-40's and pursuit pilots from the United States arrived in Australia on 12 January, but only a few of these were able to reach Java. Of the total of 40 P-40's which left Brisbane for Java in January, only 27 reached their destination. Two were destroyed on the ground at Koepang during an enemy air air attack, 5 were destroyed in similar action at Bali (off the eastern end of Java), and others were lost in combat at Bali or left behind because of engine trouble. The P-40's operated as far west as Palembang, and after the middle of February they were flying two or three combat missions a day. Receiving only first echelon maintenance, the planes were often flown while badly in need of repairs.

Ten of the P-40's were sent west during the middle of February to attack Japanese landings at Palembang. These landings were preceded by the first parachute operations to be used on a large scale in the Indies. On the morning of 14 February a total of approximately 700 enemy parachute troops were dropped near Palembang in an area of about 12 square miles, with the objectives of capturing the airport and of seizing the oil refineries before they could be destroyed by defending forces. The enemy plan was not successful, because the delayed arrival of supporting forces from the coast allowed sufficient time for the defending Dutch forces to wipe out the parachute troops and to destroy most of the refineries and installations. On the following day, however, landing forces proceeded up the Moesi River and captured Palembang and its airport. Ten P-40's could do little to hamper the landing of troops from 40 vessels. After this mission, the operating strength of pursuit planes in Java was reduced to less than 20 P-40's.

The A-24's in Australia were even later in reaching Java than were the P-40's. Three squadrons were organized and were prepared to make the flight northward. Under the command of Capt. Edward N. Backus, the 91st Squadron by February had flown via Charleville, Cloncurry, and Daly Waters to Darwin, and on 9 and 11 February the planes left in two flights for Koepang. The threat of enemy occupation of Timor prevented the 16th and 17th Squadrons from leaving Australia.

When the 11 A-24's of the 91st Squadron arrived in Java, their pilots and gunners found that more than 1,000 Javanese natives, under the direction of two Dutch officers, had been building an airfield on what was formerly riceland. Bamboo mats were spread over the soft field and covered with 4 inches of dirt. Several A-24's bogged down in the mud and had to be lifted out by main strength. With only two qualified mechanics available, 4 days were required to put 7 A-24's in combat condition. On 18 February the 7 planes assembled at Malang for refueling and bomb-loading. On the next day the Japanese were given an effective demonstration of the A-24 in action.

At Malang the planes were loaded and were awaiting orders to attack a convoy of troops approaching Den Pasar on Bali; at approximately 1245 the air-raid alarm sounded. Orders were issued for the planes to be placed back in revetments. In the confusion, however, two pilots received orders to take off. Avoiding enemy fighters by staying between two clouds, the pilots flew to Bali and broke out over the harbor, where a cruiser and a transport were sighted as perfect targets. The lack of antiaircraft fire indicated the surprise of the Japanese as the two planes dived upon the vessels. Direct hits by 110-pound bombs and near misses with 660-pound bombs, which penetrated below the line of armor plate before exploding, combined to sink both vessels.

The A-24's returned safely to Malang.

19 February

Throughout the afternoon of 19 February heavy bombers took off from Malang and Madioen to bomb enemy ships nearing Bali. The attacks were continued on the following day, with all available forces participating. Seven A-24's were escorted by 16 P-40's in one of the few "joint" actions of the air units. While a considerable amount of damage was inflicted on enemy vessels, the Japanese continued to stream ashore on the small island and to prepare the airfield at Den Pasar for operations.

The 19th of February was something of a field day for the Japanese throughout the NEI area. In addition to their operations at Bali, they effected landings at Dilli in Portuguese Timor and also carried their blows to the continent of Australia. Timor was of particular importance to Allied air operations in the Indies, for the ferrying of pursuit planes and dive bombers to Java depended upon the airfield at Koepang, Dutch Timor. No alternate landing field was available in the 1,300-mile stretch from Darwin to Java. After Japanese occupation of Dilli, on the northern part of the island, no more planes could be ferried from Australia. Furthermore, enemy control of the island meant control of the sea between Java and the northwestern part of Australia, which was included in the ABDA Command area.

Efforts had been made to reinforce the garrison at Koepang with Australian and American troops. A fast convoy of 4 troop ships, escorted by the Houston and the Peary, had left Darwin shortly after midnight on 15 February. About noon the convoy was sighted by 2 Japanese planes and on the next day was severely bombed. After the attack, the vessels continued in the direction of Koepang, but orders were soon received to return to Darwin. By 18 February the convoy had reached port and troops proceeded to disembark, while the 2 destroyers refueled and prepared to join the naval forces defending Bali. Only the Houston was able to clear the port before 19 February.

During this time a flight of 10 P-40's of the 33d Pursuit Squadron (Provisional) was attempting to reach Koepang from Darwin. When unfavorable weather was encountered, Maj. Floyd J. Pell, commanding the flight, ordered the planes to return to Darwin. He instructed 5 of the aircraft to patrol over Darwin while the other 5 were refueling. At approximately 0955 a large formation of enemy bombers flew in from the south, surprising the defending forces by attacking from an unexpected quarter. Major Pell immediately had the extra tanks removed from the P-40's on the ground, and led the planes into the air where they rejoined the remaining 5 P-40's for interception of the bombers. The total attacking forces numbered approximately 72 bombers and 36 fighters; nevertheless, the 10 P-40's attempted to penetrate the formations. One enemy bomber was shot down and others were damaged, while Major Pell and 3 other pilots of his squadron lost their lives in the action.

Such an overwhelming force of bombers assured the Japanese of free range in attacking any target in the area. They were able to destroy the airport, warehouses, docks, and virtually every vessel in the harbor, including the Peary. The entire city was strafed and set afire. Aircraft losses in the air and on the ground included 11 P-40's, 6 Hudsons, and 1 LB-30. Destruction throughout the city was so severe that by nightfall the entire area was ordered evacuated, and both civilians and certain military forces prepared to move south. No further enemy attacks were needed to convince officials that Darwin could not be used as a supply and transshipment base for forces in the Netherlands East Indies.

The Fall of Java

By this time the Japanese were driving on Java from three directions. The great fortress of Singapore had fallen on 15 February, simultaneously with Japanese occupation of Palembang. From this point the enemy could easily bomb the Dutch naval base at Batavia, only 260 air miles away, and Soerabaja, 675 miles away. In addition to attacks from the west, Japanese air forces on Borneo and Celebes were pounding Java from the north. For the third prong of the assault, the enemy was now in possession of Timor and of Bali, just off the eastern end of Java. From 3 February, when the first air attacks were made on Java, the Allied air forces were never free to operate according to their own plans. The little maintenance and repair work which could be undertaken had to be done at night, and planes had to be refueled and loaded with bombs by morning. Only by putting the bombers into the air could destruction on the ground be avoided. This constant operation of planes increased the wear on motors and made operational losses higher than they would have been otherwise. By 24 February the American air strength in Java had been reduced to 20 heavy bombers, 7 A-24's, and 16 P-40's, of which only 10 heavy bombers, 4 A-24's, and 13 P-40's were in commission.

In view of the rapidly diminishing supply of aircraft and the slight chance of aerial reinforcements, officials of the ABDA Command had already become convinced that further defense of Java was hopeless. Initial surveys had been made for continuing operations from India and Australia, and plans were made for evacuating some of the American troops from Java. By 20 February all aircraft which could not be used in combat were evacuating nonessential clerical forces and military personnel not required for the operation of remaining aircraft. Certain Air Corps reinforcements which had arrived in Australia at the beginning of February, destined for Java, were placed in another convoy and diverted to India, since General Brett felt that the Air Corps troops already in Java were sufficient to operate the planes then available or likely to be available.

On 23 February General Wavell received orders from London to leave Java and set up headquarters elsewhere. At the same time General Brereton and a small staff of officers left in two heavy bombers for India, where they were to build up an air force to oppose the Japanese drive through Burma. General Brett, on the other hand, flew to Melbourne, where he assumed command of all U. S. Army troops in Australia. The ABDA Command was officially dissolved at noon, 25 February, at which time the Dutch took over the direction of further resistance against the Japanese.

It was expected that the Dutch forces would continue to defend their territory, but they were not left entirely without aid. Many British and American troops still remained in the islands. Gen. George C. Marshall, Chief of Staff of the U. S. Army, particularly desired that the American forces in Java continue to operate as long as possible. For this reason, all American combat crews with minimum maintenance personnel and ground fighting forces were ordered to remain, even though the ABDA Command was dissolved. Colonel Eubank was left in command of the air forces. Headquarters of the V Bomber Command moved to Djogjakarta, the field at Malang was destroyed, and forces were regrouped for the last-ditch stand, which proved to be of only 1 week's duration.

Meanwhile, General Brett in Australia sought for means to aid the troops remaining in Java. While the transfer of heavy bombers was suspended, there was still a bare chance that a large number of P-40's might turn the tide of the battle. The convoy which had sailed from Australia for India included the Seawitch, carrying 27 crated P-40's, and the aircraft carrier Langley with 32 assembled P-40's, 30 pilots, and 12 crewmen on board. Upon receiving assurances from Dutch officials that protection would be provided, General Brett directed that the 2 vessels be diverted to Java. Unfortunately, the 59 P-40's were never able to get into combat. The ill-fated Langley was sunk by enemy aircraft on 27 February within 100 miles of Tjilatjap, Java. The Seawitch reached Tjilatjap on the following day, only to find that the Japanese were preparing to overrun the island, after having emerged victoriously from a fierce naval battle in the Java Sea. The 27 P-40's were reported to have been destroyed in their crates in order to prevent their falling into enemy hands.

The naval battle had developed on 27 February, when Allied air and naval units attempted to stop a Japanese armada of more than 80 vessels approaching Java from the northeast. Enemy escort forces, possessing overwhelming odds, were able to hold Allied vessels off from the convoy. All available LB-30's, B-17's, A-24's and P-40's were thrown into the operation, but clouds often obscured the targets and a complete estimate of damage could not be made. Because some difficulty was encountered in distinguishing Allied from enemy vessels, airmen were ordered in the latter part of the battle to attack only transports. Allied naval forces suffered the loss of 5 cruisers and 6 destroyers. Several enemy cruisers, destroyers, and transports were set on fire. Undeterred in their objectives, the Japanese on the night of 28 February effected landings at 2 points on the northern coast of Java. On the next day the few remaining naval units of the U. S. Asiatic Fleet were forced to withdraw to the south, and the American air forces flew their last combat missions in Java.

Final missions against Japanese transports along the northern coast were completed on the morning of March 1. By then the number of B-17's in commission was reduced to 2. Four heavy bombers, unable to take to the air, were destroyed on the ground at Djogjakarta. The P-40's, joined in their last mission by 6 Brewsters and 5 Hurricanes, returned to their hitherto secret field and were placed in dispersal positions. Japanese bombers soon appeared over the field, and by flying low found the P-40's. At the conclusion of a heavy bombing and strafing attack, every pursuit plane had been destroyed. Approximately 25 officers and 60 men who had been operating the planes then made their way to Djogjakarta, where plans were being laid for evacuation of remaining air force personnel. Under cover of darkness a 75-vehicle convoy was sent to Tjilatjap, last remaining port in Dutch hands; troops were then reloaded into vessels for the hazardous trip to Australia.

During the next 3 days every plane which could be made to fly was sent to Australia with loads of military personnel and Dutch civilians. Combat planes, thought to be incapable of flying, were ingeniously repaired and held together long enough for the trip to Broome, Australia. As the last plane cleared the field in Java, Dutch forces began to destroy all installations and to blow up all landing fields in order to deny their immediate use to the enemy.

The evacuation was not allowed to proceed unchallenged by the Japanese. Shortly before noon on 3 March, when the harbor at Broome was jammed with flying boats and the airfield covered with American, British, and Dutch planes, approximately 12 Zeros swooped over the harbor and airfield, firing at every available target and meeting no opposition except from one .30-cal. gun on the ground. A large number of deaths occurred among Dutch women and children crowded into flying boats. An incoming B-24 carried 20 Air Corps men to their death when it was shot down. Two other B-24's and 2 B-17's were lost on the ground. Dutch losses included 6 planes, while 3 British and 1 Australian aircraft were destroyed. The Japanese also attacked

Wyndham, a coastal town to the north of Broome. The only known enemy loss in these raids was 1 Zero.

Formal resistance in Java continued for only a few days longer, although guerrilla activities continued for many months after the end of formal communications with the outside world on 7 March. Elements of the Far East Air Force, redesignated on 5 February as the Fifth Air Force, had spent 2 months in the Netherlands East Indies and had finally been driven out by overwhelming Japanese air superiority. In many respects the fighting in the Indies duplicated the experience of American air units in the Philippines. Losses in aircraft on the ground had been unusually heavy, but such losses did not result from a lack of experience in dispersal and camouflage procedures. Every possible precaution was taken to protect planes on the ground, but losses were inevitable because of inadequate warning and communication systems and lack of antiaircraft artillery. Above all, the almost complete absence of planes for intercepting low-flying enemy aircraft made losses on the ground inevitable. Under such circumstances, the most effective means of protection was to put planes into the air, though such a procedure naturally added to the burden of the limited maintenance personnel and facilities. Even with extensive use of this method of protection, 65 planes were lost on the ground during the Java operations.

While destroying the striking power of the Far East Air Force, Japanese air units had moved into advance bases, taking up positions which tended to encircle the defending forces. In this manner the enemy was able to isolate Allied ground units and to prevent sizable reinforcements from reaching them. The Japanese were not novices in the art of warfare, and they demonstrated in their initial assault on Oahu, in the Philippine campaign, and in the Indies that aerial striking power was a primary weapon. In order to combat the Japanese in this kind of warfare, the American airmen who had been driven from the Philippines and Java now had the task of building up a strong air force in Australia.

WITHDRAWAL TO AUSTRALIA

Long before the fall of the Netherlands East Indies, enemy forces were penetrating Australian territory in the Bismarck Archipelago, threatening an advance upon the continent from the northeast. Aerial bombardment of Rabaul, New Britain, had begun on 16 January. Four days later the five slow Wirraways, which constituted Australian air defense forces in this area, were destroyed when they attempted to intercept more than 100 enemy planes. Following closely upon heavy air attacks, the Japanese landed strong invasion forces at Rabaul on 22 January and soon drove the Australian garrison of 1,400 men from their positions. Landings were also made in the northern Solomons, while positions throughout the Bismarck Archipelago were shelled and bombed. Lae, Madang, and Salamaua in New Guinea, the Admiralty Islands, and New Ireland were all attacked before the end of January. Extending their range still farther, the Japanese on 3 February bombed Port Moresby, capital of Papua, only 334 miles from the northern tip of Australia.

To provide for the aerial defense of New Guinea, New Britain, and the whole of Australia except Darwin (which was a part of the ABDA Command Area), the Royal Australian Air Force in January had a total of only 43 operational aircraft—29 Hudsons, 14 Catalinas, and no fighter planes. Wirraways were available, but being only advanced training planes, they were ineffective in combat. American P-40's and A-24's, unable to reach Java, were stationed in the northwestern part of Australia, thereby relieving RAAF planes for protection of other areas. A dwindling handful of Hudsons and Catalinas and 1 antiaircraft battery at Port Moresby provided the aerial defense for this strategic point. The eastern coast of Australia was essentially without aerial defense or striking power until the arrival of 12 B-17's in the latter part of February.

Heavy bombers which arrived from the United States via the South Pacific route were ferried on to Java until almost the very end of formal resistance there, but the 12 B-17's which arrived in Townsville on 18 and 19 February were not intended for participation in the Java campaign. Under the command of Maj. Richard H. Carmichael, the flight was composed of crews from the 22d Bombardment Squadron and the 88th Reconnaissance Squadron, some of whom had flown into Oahu during the Japanese attack on 7 December. After flying 168 missions out of Hawaii in 2 months, the planes were attached to a naval task force which was moving south to protect the supply line to Australia. While still a part of the task force, the squadron flew long reconnaissance and bombing missions from Townsville for more than a month without the aid of ground crews. In the absence of fighter and antiaircraft protection the planes had to be dispersed into the interior of Australia, thereby necessitating two hops—from the interior to Townsville, thence to an advance base—before take-off could be made on an actual mission.

Four days after their arrival in Australia, with only 6 B-17's in combat condition, this squadron carried out the first American bombardment of Rabaul, which was rapidly developing into a major enemy base. On account of unfavorable weather the full extent of damage to the Japanese garrison could not be determined, but at least 1 large cargo vessel was sunk, another damaged, and 3 or 4 Zeros shot down. Returning from the target, one plane ran out of gas and was forced to make a belly-landing approximately 200 miles from Port Moresby. Similar missions were flown thereafter as often as the condition of planes and crews allowed.

Other aerial reinforcements arriving from the United States were of no immediate aid in the defense of Australia, but eventually they were to provide the bulk of a new air force. More than 10,000 Air Corps officers and men were scheduled to sail from San Francisco to Brisbane during February. Among the units which arrived on the 25th of the month were the 22d and 38th Bombardment Groups (M), the 3d Bombardment Group (L), 3 squadrons of the 35th Pursuit Group (I), and the 35th, 36th, and 46th Air Base Groups. These were followed in less than 2 weeks by the 8th Pursuit Group (I) and the 22d Air Base Group. The 3d Bombardment Group brought 15 A-24's as part of its equipment, but the flying echelons and planes of the 2 medium bombardment groups and the 35th Pursuit Group could not be shipped until planes were available in the United States. From these units--substantial in numbers but deficient in equipment--and from the decimated units evacuating Java, General Brett had the task of building an air force powerful enough to halt the Japanese advance and large enough to defend a continent three-fourths the size of Europe.

AUSTRALIA
RUSTED AREAS

Indian Ocean

South Pacific Ocean

Coral Sea

Arafura Sea

Timor Sea

Tasman Sea

Australia as a Base for Operations

The decision to develop an American air force in Australia was not made because the continent was an ideal place for such an undertaking, but because the tactical situation left no alternative. The continent possessed natural barriers to operation which were to challenge the ingenuity and try the patience of American airmen. Long distances, extensive desert regions, and inadequate transportation and communication facilities created perplexing logistical problems. Radio, telephone, and telegraph systems were more than overloaded with wartime traffic. The railroads, mostly single-track and complicated by five different gauges, were not capable of meeting the full transportation needs of the Allied forces. American airmen had to depend largely upon "truck-tractor-trailers" for moving crated aircraft from ports to erection centers, but many of the roads were merely graded or covered with crushed rock and were often impassable during rainy weather. Under such circumstances, the importance of air transportation was paramount.

American forces made maximum use of Australian facilities, goods, and services, but a considerable stepping up of industrial production was necessary before all demands could be met. Even then, the undertaking of large-scale operations was dependent upon a line of supply extending across the Pacific from the United States. The fact that Australia was 7,000 miles from North America created problems of defense in the area between the two continents. Since the fall of Java, planes flying to the Southwest Pacific were entirely dependant upon the South Pacific route, and necessarily the garrisoning of the chain of islands leading down from Hawaii to Australia constituted a first claim upon both air and ground forces available for the Pacific. The line of supply first had to be made secure.

New Caledonia, occupying a strategic position east of Australia, received a larger share of Pacific defense forces than any of the smaller islands along this line. In February a task force under the command of Brig. Gen. Alexander M. Patch proceeded from the United States to Australia, where it was reloaded before making the final leg of the voyage to New Caledonia. During the first week in March, arrangements were made for a naval task force to provide protection for the movement of the convoy to Noumea, New Caledonia. On the night of 6 March the force left for its destination, while final plans were made for carrier-based attacks on enemy ships and installations in the Bismarck-Solomons area. When information was received on 7 March that a Japanese convoy was moving toward New Guinea and on the following day that 11 warships had begun to shell Lae and Salamaua, the original plans were changed and an assault on these newest enemy attempts was scheduled for 10 March.

While the New Caledonia force continued eastward, 2 U. S. carriers of the naval task force sailed into the Gulf of Papua and launched more than 100 planes across the mountains of New Guinea to attack enemy forces at Lae and Salamaua. Eight B-17's from Townsville and a number of RAAF Hudsons also participated, concentrating on additional vessels which were sighted 25 miles off the coast. With the loss of only 1 scout bomber, the combined forces sank a reported total of 5 merchant ships, 2 heavy cruisers, 1 light cruiser, and 1 destroyer; and damaged 2 destroyers, 2 gunboats, 1 minelayer, and 1 seaplane tender. Though hampered by these attacks, the Japanese continued with the occupation of Lae and Salamaua—a move which was viewed by General Brett as preliminary to the first phase of operations against the northeast coast of Australia or possibly New Caledonia and the Solomons. The New Caledonia task force reached Nounea safely on 12 March and, in cooperation with other forces on the island, prepared to hold New Caledonia against Japanese aggression.

American Air Strength in Australia

The task of defending Australia, with its 12,000 miles of coastline, was not simple. Because of the flexibility of enemy carrier-based operations, any point on the continent was subject to attack. In view of this situation, General Brett planned to station air units in each of seven widely separated areas—Darwin, Townsville, Brisbane, Melbourne, Adelaide, Perth, and Sydney. Forces necessary to provide the defensive and offensive air strength in these areas were estimated to include 3 heavy bombardment groups of 4 squadrons each, 3 medium bombardment groups, 3 light bombardment groups, 6 pursuit groups, 3 transport groups, 2 air depot groups, 2 aviation engineer battalions, and the necessary service organizations. In contrast with these estimated needs, the number of tactical units allotted to Australia included only 3 pursuit groups, and 1 light, 2 medium, and 2 heavy bombardment groups. As was the case throughout the AAF at this time, the demand for combat units far exceeded the supply.

Moreover, at the beginning of March 1942 there was a vast difference between allotted strength and actual strength of air units in Australia. Even those units which had arrived from the United States in February were not in condition to be placed into combat, and most of the tactical squadrons were without aircraft. Organizational, training, and supply problems all confronted General Brett as he surveyed the possibilities of developing a strong air force on the continent. Training activities were undertaken by newly-arrived squadrons as soon as equipment and facilities allowed.

The month of March was devoted to the reorganization of forces evacuated from Java and the preparation of all units for combat operations. On 5 March the Abbekerk arrived at Fremantle, after a precarious voyage from Tjilatjap, Java, carrying part of the ground echelons of the 7th Bombardment Group and part of the 19th Bombardment Group. These officers and men, along with others who had arrived at Broome, gradually made their way across the continent by train, air transportation, and other means to Melbourne, where they were placed in a rest camp for a few days. Remnants of the 7th and 19th Groups in Australia were reorganized as the 19th Group on 14 March, with Lt. Col. Kenneth B. Hobson assuming command. The new group was composed of Headquarters and Headquarters Squadron, the 28th, 30th, and 93d Bombardment Squadrons, and the 40th Reconnaissance Squadron, the latter including the 12 B-17's and their crews which had been operating from Townsville under the naval task force. Because of the time required to build up the allotted strength of heavy bombers, approximately 2 months elapsed before the entire 19th Group could again get into operations.

Availability of aircraft affected also the 27th and 3d Bombardment Groups. Since the production of light bombers in the United States did not permit the maintenance of two groups in Australia, the 27th was absorbed by the 3d. The reorganized 3d Group, under the command of Lt. Col. John H. Davies, proved to be one of the most versatile units in Australia. When no replacements were available for the A-24's which were lost in operations out of Port Moresby, the group acquired a number of B-25's which had been ordered by the Dutch but could not be used by them. Two squadrons of B-25's and A-24's were then rotated between Port Moresby and Charters Towers, about 70 miles inland from Townsville. With the attrition of the remaining A-24's, A-20's were made available as replacements, making a total of three types of aircraft which the 3d Bombardment Group had to operate and maintain.

The three pursuit groups, having absorbed the 3d, 17th, and 20th Pursuit Squadrons (Provisional), were getting into position in three of the vital areas of Australia by mid-March. First of the three groups to begin combat operations, the 49th, commanded by Lt. Col. Paul B. Wurtsmith and equipped with P-40's, moved to the RAAF airdrome at Darwin. The 8th Pursuit Group, equipped with P-39's, was preparing to take up its position in the Brisbane area; while the 35th Group, equipped with P-400's,* was going into position in the Sydney area.

*/ The P-400 was an export model of the P-39, modified for British use.

The three additional pursuit groups requested by General Brett could not be provided.

Similarly, there was a scarcity of transport planes. Authority was granted for activation of the 21st and 22d Transport Squadrons in March, but units had to be equipped almost entirely with planes available from sources other than the AAF. Only 3 C-39's and 2 C-47's could be sent immediately from the United States to Australia. A miscellaneous assortment of about 15 planes unfit for combat duty were already being used for transport purposes, and every Australian commercial plane was pressed into service. Acquisition of a few aircraft which the NEI government could no longer use soon raised the total transport aircraft to 36, but even this number fell far short of requirements.

Flights to the Philippines

With American, Dutch, and Australian forces pooling their resources, essentially the same condition which had existed in Java was now taking shape in Australia. There was need for long-range planning which could be assured only by integration of the various forces under one controlling office. To meet this demand, plans were made late in February for bringing Gen. Douglas MacArthur from the Philippines to become supreme commander of forces in the Southwest Pacific, with headquarters in Australia.

On the rainy evening of 11 March, General MacArthur, his wife and small son, and a number of staff officers left Corregidor in two speedy PT boats. Taking separate routes, the two boats darted out of Manila Bay and then proceeded to Mindanao. At the same time, four B-17's of the 40th Reconnaissance Squadron at Townsville prepared for a flight to Del Monte Field. Three of the planes succeeded in taking off from Australia, carrying a cargo of medical supplies and other items needed by the forces on Bataan. At the blacked-out field on Mindanao, not far from Japanese forces at Davao, General MacArthur and his party boarded the planes for the trip south. The flight was executed without mishap; after landing on the coast on 17 March, members of the party were flown inland where they entrained for Melbourne. At Canberra, Prime Minister John Curtin announced the arrival of General MacArthur and also the selection of General Brett to head Allied air forces.

Approximately 10 days later, part of the Australian Imperial Forces which had been serving under Gen. Sir Thomas Blamey in the Middle East returned to boost Allied forces in Australia. At the same time, the 8th Air Base Group and the 43d Bombardment Group, minus combat crews, arrived to round out the units authorized for General Brett's command. Having laid the groundwork for the organization and operation of the individual American units, General Brett could now turn to the larger task of organizing the Allied Air Forces in Australia, but he--like General MacArthur--was hampered somewhat by lack of a formal declaration of his authority.

The relative stalemate on the command level during this period was not entirely duplicated on the operational level. A number of successful evacuation flights had been made to the Philippines throughout March. Approximately a week after General MacArthur's arrival in Australia three more B-17's evacuated President Emanuel Quezon, his family, and certain officials of the Philippine government. Several other heavy bombers carried supplies to Del Monte and brought personnel to Australia on the return flights. The success of these flights gave rise to a daring operational plan early in April which was designed to inflict as much damage as possible on Japanese installations in the Philippines and at the same time to bolster the morale of defending forces in those islands.

Plans had to be made hurriedly, for by 9 April the American and Filipino troops on Bataan were overwhelmed, leaving only the fortress of Corregidor and a small force on Mindanao. On the same day crews of the 3d Bombardment Group took 11 new B-25's from Charters Towers to Brisbane in order to pick up bomb bay tanks. To those former members of the 27th Bombardment Group who had been "bouncing around the skies" for several months in A-24's, the B-25 "felt like a ball of fire" until they became accustomed to its extra speed and power. The 11 B-25's and 3 B-17's assembled at the RAAF airdrome at Darwin early on the morning of 11 April. While crews ate a hurried breakfast, planes were prepared for the long, over-water hop to Mindanao. Take-off was made by all aircraft with the exception of 1 B-25. Brig. Gen. Ralph Royce flew in the lead B-17, piloted by Capt. Frank P. Bostrom. The first flight of 5 B-25's was led by Col. John H. Davies and the second flight by Capt. Herman F. Lovery.

Twelve hours after leaving Darwin the last plane landed safely at Del Monte, where the aircraft were to operate as long as ammunition and fuel held out or as long as the Japanese would allow. Early on the morning of 12 April the two flights of B-25's bombed Cebu, sinking several vessels which were landing troops and interfering with blockade runners. One B-17 obtained hits on surface craft, while another scoured the seas for enemy concentrations, flew over Corregidor, and then bombed Nichols Field. The third B-17, undergoing maintenance at Del Monte, was seriously damaged by enemy air attacks on the field. Immediately upon the return of the other B-17's, crews rushed preparations for another mission. Before the planes could take off, however, enemy air attacks were resumed. One B-17 was destroyed with a direct hit, and the remaining 2 were damaged.

Crews spent the next 15 hours preparing the B-17's for the return flight to Australia, while the B-25's continued to attack Japanese installations. Cebu was again attacked on the afternoon of 12 April and on the following morning. Davao shipping and air installations were also attacked on the morning and afternoon of 13 April. Bomb bay tanks were then reinstalled in the B-25's, and planes were loaded with personnel evacuated from Bataan. On the day before the fall of Bataan, all pursuit planes had carried out as many men as could be loaded into the small aircraft. Prior to and during the B-17 and B-25 bombing attacks, the 4 P-40's on Mindanao, reinforced by 4 P-40's and 2 P-35's from Bataan, flew reconnaissance, escort, and attack missions.

By the morning of 14 April the return flight to Australia had been completed by 2 B-17's and 10 B-25's. In their 2 days of operation against the enemy these planes had sunk or badly damaged 4 enemy transports and scored hits and near misses on 10 others; they had also damaged Nichols Field and docks, warehouses, and other buildings at Davao and Cebu.

General MacArthur's promise to send aid to the Philippines had seen its initial fulfillment, but in a sense, the raid was only a token effort. It could not be repeated, for the Japanese on Mindanao immediately began to close in on American airfields. The plan to bomb the enemy in the Islands had been hastily devised and hurriedly executed, and crew members of the B-25's were not entirely accustomed to the planes or to each other. But there could be no doubt that both the native population and the American and Filipino troops still resisting the enemy were heartened.

The Southwest Pacific Command

On 18 April General MacArthur formally assumed command of the Southwest Pacific Area. Two days later, from Allied Headquarters at Melbourne, the commanders under General MacArthur were announced as follows:

Gen. Sir Thomas Blamey, Commander of Allied Land Forces
Lt. Gen. George H. Brett, Commander of Allied Air Forces
Vice Adm. Herbert F. Leary, Commander of Allied Naval Forces
Lt. Gen. Jonathan M. Wainwright, Commander of Forces in the Philippines
Maj. Gen. Julian F. Barnes, Commander of U. S. Army Forces in Australia

As Supreme Commander in the Southwest Pacific Area, General MacArthur's responsibilities were manifold. He was directed to hold Australia as a base for future offensive action, to check the Japanese advance toward the continent, to maintain the position of American forces in the Philippines, and to protect land, sea, and air communications within the Southwest Pacific Area. [General MacArthur was not responsible for the internal administration of forces under his command; nor was he responsible for grand strategy, which came under the jurisdiction of the Combined Chiefs of Staff, or for operational strategy, which fell within the province of the U. S. Joint Chiefs of Staff.]

By agreement of the governments of Australia, New Zealand, the United Kingdom, the Netherlands, and the United States, the entire Pacific Theater was designated as an area of U. S. strategic responsibility. The theater was divided into three large areas: the Southwest Pacific, the Southeast Pacific, and the Pacific Ocean, the latter being subdivided into the North, Central, and South Pacific Areas. The South Pacific Area, which included New Zealand and New Caledonia, was set up as a naval command under the Commander in Chief of the Pacific Ocean Area, who was directed to maintain the line of communications between the United States and the Southwest Pacific, to contain Japanese forces within the Pacific Theater, to support operations in the Southwest Pacific Area, and to prepare for amphibious offensives to be launched from the South and Southwest Pacific Areas.

General Brett officially assumed command of the Allied Air Forces in the Southwest Pacific on 20 April, with the following assignments to his command: complete control of all Air Corps tactical units and associated service elements of the U. S. Army then in Australia, and operational control of all service squadrons (excluding training units) of the RAAF and of the Royal Netherlands East Indies Army Air Force. Staff positions, as announced on 2 May, were equally divided between the Australians and Americans.

A shortage of qualified Air Corps personnel extended down to the smallest unit and had a direct effect upon operational efficiency. Some units had been sent from the United States before reaching their authorized strength. Once in Australia, squadrons were soon depleted by casualties, flying fatigue, and dengue fever. Replacements to meet all these demands were not immediately available, and forces in the Southwest Pacific could look forward to relief only when such action would not be detrimental to forces in other theaters and to the training program in the United States.

Considerations of mobility called for an air force command which would remain in an area so long as combat units were there and then move forward with the advancing units. To meet this demand, General Brett established Air Command Number 1, under Brig. Gen. Albert L. Sneed at Darwin, and Air Command Number 2, under Brig. Gen. Martin F. Scanlon at Townsville.

Supply and Maintenance

Concurrent with the organization of the Allied command, a system of supply and maintenance services was evolved from the somewhat cumbersome procedures which characterized the first few months of the war. Steps were taken both in the United States and in Australia to eliminate some of the undesirable features of the supply system, but even after 5 months of war, units were still arriving in Australia without their equipment. Some of the equipment, moreover, was in no condition to be used when it finally arrived. Deck-loaded materiel was damaged by the corrosive action of salt spray, and some pursuit planes--taken directly from maneuvers and shipped without depot inspection--had to be repaired in Australia. Remedial action was taken to correct this situation and also to prevent aircraft and other supplies designated for the Southwest Pacific from being removed from cargo vessels at intermediate steps in the South Pacific islands.

The chief innovation in the organization of supply and maintenance services was the divorce of air base groups from their original assignments to tactical units and the consequent assumption of an area responsibility by these groups. Before this reassignment was made, however, all service units of the American air forces in Australia were organized under a new command. On 27 April the United States Army Air Services was created as an integral part of the Allied Air Forces, with Maj. Gen. Rush B. Lincoln as commander.

As was the case with combat units, the service units were faced with the problems of an insufficient number of personnel, a shortage of trained personnel, and an inadequate number of units to meet operational demands. In some instances, personnel had to be drawn from tactical organizations to create service units for immediate use. A small number of factory representatives--civilian technical specialists--aided considerably by advising and training inexperienced members of air depot and materiel units.

The 4th Air Depot Group, by dividing its 41 officers and 617 enlisted men between three widely separated locations, was attempting in April to carry out functions which normally would require three such groups. At Footscray, Victoria, the group was operating a central supply depot; branch supply depots were set up at Brisbane and at Wagga Wagga in New South Wales, where a major repair depot was to be temporarily located. Work was also in progress on a permanent repair and supply depot at Tocumwal. In addition, the group was charged with the supervision of aircraft assembly facilities at Amberley and Geelong. On 1 May authorization was granted for activation of an additional air depot group, the 81st; but personnel and equipment were to be taken from supplies available in Australia.

Having only the 1 air depot group at its disposal at the end of April, the Army Air Services had to use the 6 air base groups as additional branch supply depots. The groups were also assigned the task of rendering general service to all tactical units in the respective areas, which involved the maintenance of all types of aircraft. For example, the 35th Air Base Group, assigned to the Townsville area, had to be able to service the A-20's, A-24's, and B-25's of the 3d Bombardment Group; the B-26's of the 22d Bombardment Group; the B-17's of the 19th Bombardment Group; the P-39's of the 8th Pursuit Group; and any of the odd assortment of planes used by the transport squadrons.

Providing aviation fuel was one of the major concerns of supply units in Australia. Difficulties of storage and transportation on the continent, as well as duplication of effort in requisitioning the supplies, called for a considerable amount of untangling. To begin with, stocks of 100-octane gasoline in Australia were relatively small and not strategically located. Most of the storage capacity was in the southern part of the continent, thus requiring bulk shipments from the United States to be unloaded at southern ports. Rail shipment thence to tactical units in the north was almost out of the question, for every change in railroad gauge meant the pumping of fuel from one tank car into another. Transshipment therefore had to be made largely by water, but this arrangement called for an enormous number of fuel drums to be sent from the United States.

In connection with its maintenance, supply, weather, and other services prerequisite for the operation of an effective air force in Australia, the Army Air Services also contributed to the development of suitable airdromes and landing fields in the Southwest Pacific Area. The entire program of air-base projects was delayed by the lack of proper tools and equipment, the scarcity of local labor, and the lack of sufficient aviation engineering battalions. The 808th, the only such battalion in Australia, throughout the spring of 1942 was busy constructing airdromes in the Northern Territory.

Reinforcement of the South Pacific

While engaged in the process of organization and establishment during the spring, Allied forces in the South and Southwest Pacific constituted only a potential threat to the enemy. The gradual reinforcement of New Zealand, New Caledonia, the New Hebrides, and the Fiji Islands, as well as Australia, was part of the Allied strategy of securing the supply line and of preparing bases for launching offensive moves against the Japanese. This necessarily slow process was conducted in the face of the southward push of the enemy, who seemed determined to cut the lines of communication between Australia and the United States.

In April, General MacArthur was requested to provide air support for the Army forces on New Caledonia, but because of enemy concentrations in the northern Solomons it was considered too late and too dangerous to attempt any direct reinforcement from Australia. Aerial protection for New Caledonia was therefore limited for the time to whatever assistance the Allied Air Forces, concentrated on the east coast of Australia, could provide. A month later, however, the ground echelon of the 69th Squadron of the 38th Bombardment Group (H), with attached ordnance platoon, was dispatched to New Caledonia from Australia. The squadron's flying echelon was still in training in the United States and was not expected to be sent to the South Pacific until the first part of June or until its training was completed.

The ground echelon of the 70th Squadron of the same group was simultaneously sent to the Fiji Islands. Other air force units totaling 664 officers and men, accompanied by 25 P-40's, were dispatched from Australia to Tongatabu, 500 miles southwest of Samoa and southernmost of the Tonga group. Additional Army and Navy forces were shipped to these islands, directly from the United States. Since the line of the Japanese advance was not entirely encompassed in either the South or the Southwest Pacific areas, a high degree of coordination was demanded of the two Allied commanders, General MacArthur in the Southwest Pacific and Vice Adm. Robert H. Ghormley in the South Pacific.

Early Operations

It was imperative that the Allied Air Forces develop a system of air intelligence which would reveal every enemy move in the vicinity of Australia and in the Bismarck Archipelago. For more than 2 months after its arrival in the latter part of February the 40th Reconnaissance Squadron, operating from Townsville, had performed most of the photographic and reconnaissance work for the American and Australian forces and also for naval task forces in that area.

The need for properly equipped photographic squadrons had been recognized not only by combat units but also by AAF headquarters. Shortly after the outbreak of war the Director of Photography was assigned 100 P-38's which were to be modified by the installation of cameras. A training program was inaugurated at Colorado Springs, and the advance flight of the first unit to be ready for operation was sent to Australia. Flight "A" of the 8th Photographic Squadron arrived on 7 April and within 9 days was in operation with its 4 F-4's (P-38E's modified with cameras and 2 additional 75-gallon tanks).

Anticipating the assignment of photographic units to all theaters, the AAF on 9 April reorganized its reconnaissance aviation. All existing reconnaissance squadrons were redesignated as bombardment squadrons and assigned as the fourth bombardment squadron of their respective groups, while the photographic section in each reconnaissance squadron was to be transferred to the group headquarters. Under an expanded program which called for the activation of 6 photographic groups between 1 July and 31 December 1942, each air force eventually was to be assigned 1 photographic group consisting of 1 mapping squadron, 2 photographic squadrons, and a group headquarters squadron. Under the reorganization of 9 April the 40th Reconnaissance Squadron—the famous "Kangaroo Squadron"—of the 19th Bombardment Group became the 435th Bombardment Squadron. All bombardment squadrons in combat condition, however, continued to fly reconnaissance missions.

For the most part, units of the Allied Air Forces were slow in reaching a stage of combat readiness, either awaiting the arrival of planes and flying personnel or awaiting the establishment of necessary facilities and services. The 43d Bombardment Group (H) and the 38th Bombardment Group (M), for example, had only their ground echelons throughout the spring. The first combat crews of the 43d Group did not begin to arrive until July, while the flying echelon of the 38th Group was left in the United States for an intensive training period with B-26's.

The other medium bombardment group in Australia, the 22d, by the latter part of April was equipped with 80 B-26's and 12 B-25's and was stationed in the Townsville area. The group was establishing a successful record in combat, although certain mechanical restrictions forced the B-26's to operate at low altitudes. Equipped with the original model B-26, the first squadron of the group started operations against Japanese targets in northern New Guinea in early April. One squadron was training for torpedo work, with 23 Navy pilots assisting in the training. The fact that most of the crews were well acquainted with the peculiarities of the B-26 and the fact that it was a new type of aircraft to the Japanese contributed to the initial success of the plane in combat operations.

Another medium bombardment type, the B-25, was being used extensively by the 3d Bombardment Group (L), along with its dwindling supply of A-24's. After absorbing the remnants of the 27th Bombardment Group (L), in March, the group carried-out its first mission on 6 April—a successful attack on the landing strip at Gasmata, New Britain—although some of the more seasoned pilots of the former 27th Group had begun to carry out missions from Port Moresby on 1 April with their A-24's escorted by P-40's from an RAAF squadron. Stationed at Charters Towers, the group performed numerous reconnaissance, patrol, and attack missions out of Port Moresby, sometimes with fighter escort but more often unescorted. A-20A's, which were made available as replacements for A-24's, had to be modified to increase their range and firing power before they could be put into action.

Like the 3d and 22d Bombardment Group, the 19th Bombardment Group was located in the Townsville area. After reorganizing at Melbourne, three squadrons had completed their move to Cloncurry in Queensland by the latter part of April, although advance flights of the squadrons were carrying-out a few patrol missions by the middle of the month. Unfavorable weather conditions, lack of spare parts and tools, and the "burned out" condition of combat crews after the Philippine and Java action all affected the operational efficiency of the group. Patrol and bombing missions were carried out almost daily, despite the fact that squadrons were sometimes able to get only one plane into the air.

Until the flying echelon of the 43d Group began to arrive in the late summer of 1942, the 19th Group carried the entire heavy bombardment burden in the Southwest Pacific Area.

Operations by bombardment aircraft—light, medium, and heavy—were carried out as often as the condition of the planes would allow. Advance bases at Horn Island, Port Moresby, and Darwin provided refueling and loading facilities which increased the range of aircraft and enabled them to penetrate deeply into enemy-held territory. Lae, Salamaua, Finschaven, and other points along the northeast coast of New Guinea were hit regularly. Rabaul, with its several Japanese airdromes and large concentrations of shipping, was one of the most consistently bombed targets in the Southwest Pacific. In addition, Allied planes were put over such distant enemy positions as Kavieng in New Ireland, Buka and Bougainville in the Solomon Islands, and Koepang and Kendari in the Netherlands East Indies. Enemy shipping was hit in harbors, as well as throughout the Bismarck Sea, Dampier Strait, and waters nearer to Australia.

Until the fall of Corregidor and the end of formal resistance in the Philippines on 6 May, heavy bombers from Australia continued to evacuate personnel on Mindanao. The last successful evacuation flight was made in a B-24 piloted by Capt. Alvin J. Mueller. The plane departed from Del Monte shortly before midnight on 29 April, just 3 hours after its arrival, and carried its load of passengers to Batchelor Field, south of Darwin. On 5 May, Captain Mueller again flew to Mindanao with a heavy cargo of mail, ammunition and other supplies.

For 3 hours the plane circled Del Monte, Valencia, and Maramag fields; but no runway light appeared and a landing could not be made. Running out of gas before reaching Australia, the plane was forced down near an island, where the crew remained until rescued by submarine. No more evacuation flights could be attempted, for by this time the outnumbered and exhausted forces under Lt. Gen. Jonathan Wainwright had surrendered after 28 days of siege which included more than 100 bombing attacks on Corregidor.

The three American fighter groups in Australia, along with one RAAF group, were engaged in defensive operations, protective cover duties, and attack missions, amply demonstrating the suitability of their redesignation early in June from "pursuit" to "fighter"—a change which was effective throughout the Army Air Forces. The 49th Fighter Group, commanded by Col. Paul B. Wurtsmith, was notably successful in operations throughout the Darwin area. Frequent enemy air attacks gave the group ample opportunity to develop the best tactics which the characteristics of the P-40 would allow. Because of its slow rate of climb and inability to operate at high levels, the plane had to be used largely in hit-and-run tactics against enemy fighters. At medium altitudes the P-40 was estimated to be 40 to 50 miles faster than the Zero fighter; above 18,000 feet, however, the performance was sluggish.

A similar experience was encountered with the P-39, although this plane was slightly later in getting into combat than the P-40. The 35th and 36th Fighter Squadrons of the 8th Group moved into Port Moresby in late April to replace the RAAF units which had been used up in operations. On 30 April the P-39's received their baptism of fire in combat with the Japanese. Lt. Col. Boyd D. "Buzz" Wagner, still suffering from an eye wound received in his last action in the Philippines, led 12 inexperienced pilots on a ground strafing mission against Lae airdrome, 180 miles north. The strafing was completed, but after withdrawing from the target the planes were engaged by 12 or 13 Zeros in a fierce low-altitude dogfight which continued about 30 miles down the coast and back again. Four Zeros were shot down in flames, 3 of them by Wagner, while 3 P-39's were lost. All 3 pilots were safe after parachuting or crash-landing on the beach. Performance of the P-39 was described as excellent, though it had the same disadvantages as the P-40.

Japanese fighter pilots had been quick to capitalize on the high operational ceiling of their planes, and American pilots were reported to have "a feeling of hopelessness in their inability to outclimb and out-maneuver the enemy." The morale of bomber crews also was affected by the necessarily small size of their efforts and by the lack of fighter protection on long missions. Other factors, such as the lack of a definite combat relief policy and the slowness with which some promotions came through, were sources of complaint; but even under all these circumstances, morale among the officers and men of the AAF in Australia was considered "good."

It was recognized both in the Southwest Pacific and at AAF headquarters that the aircraft which could be sent to Australia were barely sufficient to hold the Japanese to the line of their advancement.

Because of the small number of bombers, only harassing operations could be carried out against enemy installations. But the Allied Air Forces were taking their toll of the enemy while making preparation for the time when increased production of planes and provision of necessary personnel, facilities, and supplies would enable them to assume the offensive.

-VI-
AIR REINFORCEMENTS FOR THE ASIATIC MAINLAND

Japanese expansion in the Pacific had not been made at the expense of her older war against China, for during the early months of 1942 enemy troops were pushing through southeast Asia toward the southern approaches of China, penetrating into Burma, and threatening the vital Burma Road lifeline of China. It was felt by Allied military leaders that Japanese success in this latter objective would not only be disastrous for China but would also seriously hamper the entire Allied effort against Japan. Plans were therefore made in January for creating the China-Burma-India theater of operations, with Chinese, British, and American officials occupying command positions. Early in February Lt. Gen. Joseph W. Stilwell, former military attaché in Peiping, was appointed commander of U. S. Army Forces in the new theater.

When early in the same month Japanese penetration of the Netherlands East Indies foretold the dissolution of the ABDA Command, General Brett and General Brereton joined in urging the establishment of an air force in the India-Burma region as well as in Australia. At their instance preliminary surveys were made, and during the last week of February, while General Brett set up headquarters in Australia, General Brereton and a small group of officers flew to India.

The AVG

The decision to establish an American air force in the India-Burma region was not the first overt indication of American interest in China's defense. Voluntary assistance from individuals, lend-lease aid, and an American military mission under Brig. Gen. John Magruder had all been sent to China prior to the outbreak of the Pacific war in 1941. In 1937 the Chinese Air Force began to profit from the leadership of a retired Air Corps officer, Claire L. Chennault, a leading exponent of formation flying and an expert in fighter tactics. Under his command the Chinese force fought the Japanese until Russian entry in the European war in 1941 cut off China's main source of aircraft supply. Then, with Japanese air attacks on the Burma Road increasing the seriousness of China's position, Chennault evolved an ingenious plan in creating the First American Volunteer Group. One hundred experienced pilots and about 200 ground crewmen were enlisted, and by July 1941 the first contingent was ready to sail from the United States. One hundred obsolescent P-40's, originally allocated to Sweden, were allocated to the group through lend-lease, and an intensive training program was begun in September at Toungoo in neutral Burma.

Because of the importance of thorough training in the tactics devised by Chennault, the AVG did not get into combat until 20 December 1941. From the time of its first battle over Rangoon, the AVG--soon known as the "Flying Tigers"--ran up a remarkable record against the Japanese before being disbanded in the summer of 1942.

Throughout January and February the Tigers, operating from bases in China, won air superiority over the Burma Road and kept the important port of Rangoon open for almost 3 months after the first enemy assaults began. During their 7 months of operation the AVG provided the most heartening news to come from the Far East. In stopping the enemy push into southern China through the Salween gorge and in giving certain Chinese areas their first relief from enemy bombing, they bolstered not only Chinese but also Allied morale at a time when Allied defeats and set-backs seemed to be the order of the day.

The Tenth Air Force

Royal Air Force units had cooperated with the AVG in opposing the Japanese advance into Burma; but by the time of General Brereton's arrival in India enemy gains had been so great as to indicate not only the wisdom but even the necessity of establishing a strong American air force in the India-Burma region. Successful termination of the Malayan campaign in mid-February had enabled the Japanese to regroup their forces and to drive into Burma. British defenders were pushed back along the Salween estuary, and the fall of Martaban on 11 February proved an important victory for the Japanese in their drive to cut the Rangoon-Lashio railroad. By 27 February the railway had been cut 50 miles north of Pegu, and enemy planes had begun to raid the Andaman Islands in the Bay of Bengal. The inescapable conclusion was that Rangoon would shortly fall into Japanese hands and that Calcutta and the Bay of Bengal would undoubtedly be closed to Allied shipping. It was under these circumstances that General Brereton began to make plans for establishing the Tenth Air Force in India. At New Delhi, where headquarters had been located in order to effect better coordination with the British, General Brereton formally assumed command of the new air force on 5 March 1942.

As was the case in Australia, there was little about India—except for the tactical situation—to recommend it as a theater of operations. Perhaps its chief disadvantage was its great distance from the United States. No available sea route was less than 13,000 statute miles, and shipments from the United States required a minimum of 2 months to reach India. Even after arriving at their destination, ships could not be unloaded immediately because of limited docking space. Since ports along the Bay of Bengal could no longer be used, the few western ports were soon jammed with British and American shipping. In April, for example, it was reported that more than 200 ships were waiting to be unloaded at Bombay, some of them having stood there for 6 weeks.

Karachi, selected as the chief port of American entry, was more than 1,000 miles away from the center of combat activities. Consequently, a heavy burden was placed upon already inadequate transportation and communication systems. The poorly developed railroad system, hampered by a lack of rolling stock and the existence of four different gauges, could be of only limited usefulness to the American forces. The highway system was even less prepared to absorb part of

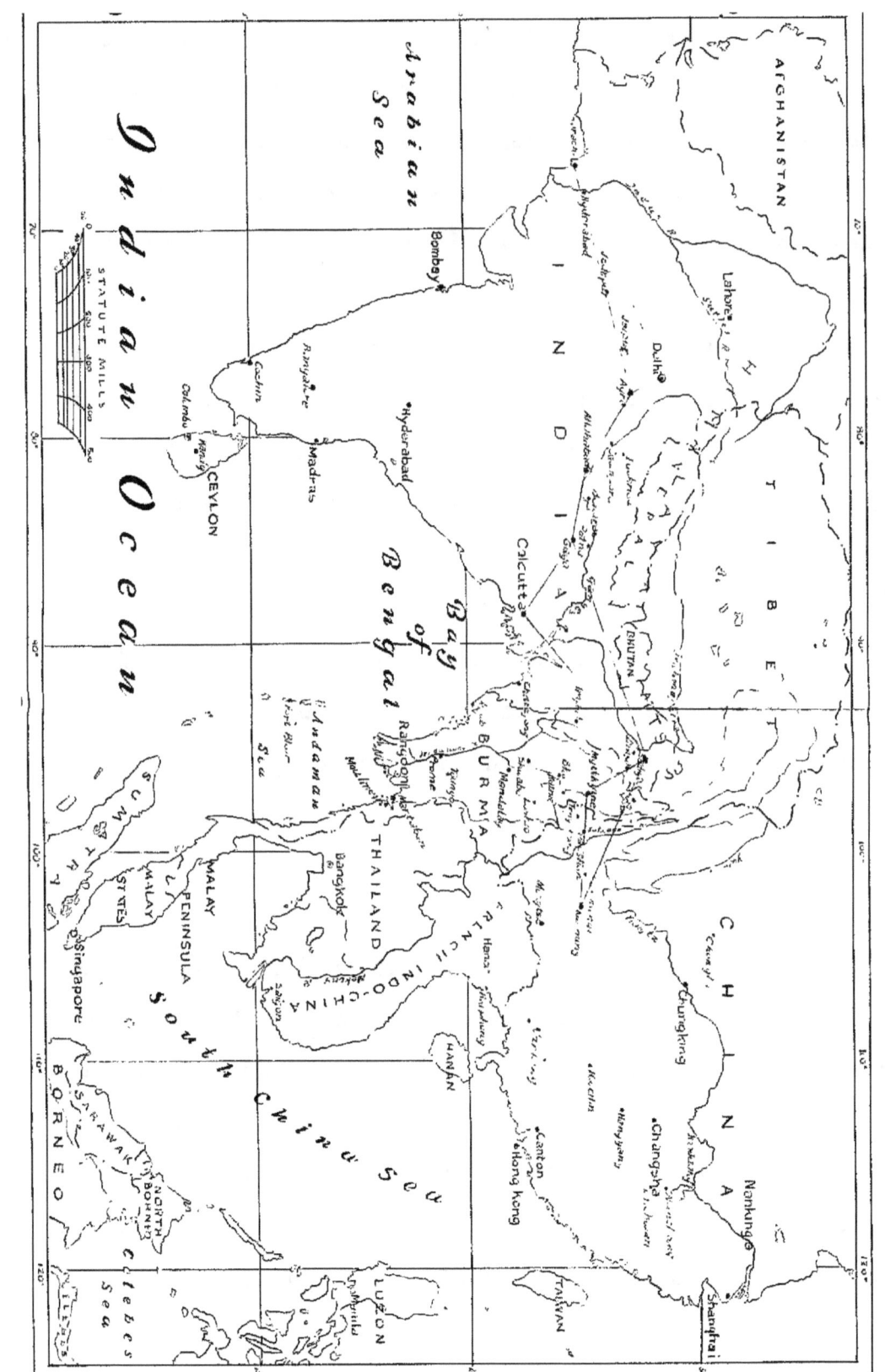
India-China Ferry Routes, 1942

the transportation burden. Narrow, poorly graded roads, largely impassable during rainy weather, made up the larger part of the system. Even if every road had been a two-lane, all-weather highway, trucks were not available for hauling large numbers of troops and supplies. A certain amount of freight could be carried on the Ganges and Brahmaputra rivers, although this means of transportation could not be fully utilized until more boats could be obtained. Development of an air transport service had to await completion of an extensive construction program, for the existing commercial fields were not strategically located and were not entirely suitable for military planes. Finally, the American forces could not depend upon the slow telephone and telegraph systems for rapid communications essential to combat. Added to these problems was the fact that India's climate, which ran to excesses in temperature and humidity, was not conducive to the highest operational efficiency of personnel or of aircraft.

Prospects for obtaining the desired personnel and equipment for the Tenth Air Force were none too bright, for demands from other theaters and the policy of concentrating first on the elimination of Germany gave India a low priority. While the Tenth Air Force was activated on 12 February 1942 at Patterson Field, Ohio, it was not until several months later that the Headquarters and Headquarters Squadron could be sent from the United States. As a nucleus for his staff, General Brereton had only the officers who had been evacuated from Java in two heavy bombers. Brig. Gen. Earl

L. Naiden was to become chief of staff, while Brig. Gen. Francis M. Brady was scheduled for command of the base at Karachi for the reception, classification, and training of incoming personnel.

The first large shipment of Air Corps troops to arrive at Karachi was the convoy sent from Australia on 22 February. Originally scheduled for Java, the troops had been diverted to India, and on 12 March they reached Karachi, after stopping for 2 days at Colombo, Ceylon. Included in this shipment were the 51st Pursuit Group, the 51st Air Base Group, and the 9th Bombardment Squadron and 88th Reconnaissance Squadron (ground echelon) of the 7th Bombardment Group. These units brought the total strength of the Tenth Air Force in India to 174 officers and 3,036 enlisted men.

Only 10 P-40's were brought in the convoy. An additional 59 P-40's on the Langley and Seawitch had started with the convoy from Australia, but at the last minute the two vessels were diverted to Java, where enemy action prevented the planes from getting into combat. While developments in Java had resulted in the loss of valuable pursuit aircraft, they provided the first heavy bombers for the Tenth Air Force when planes en route to Java via the South Atlantic route were ordered to be held in India. Thus it happened that 6 B-17's, plus the 2 bombers flown in by General Brereton and his party, and 10 P-40's constituted the initial strength of the Tenth Air Force.

Early Operational Problems

No time was wasted in getting the available aircraft into action. Even before the arrival of pursuit planes the bombers were carrying out their first "mission." Between 8 and 13 March, 7 B-17's and 1 LB-30 transported 29 tons of supplies and a battalion of native Fusiliers from Asansol in India to Magwe in Burma, and evacuated 423 civilians on return trips. Following the completion of this task, the planes returned to Karachi for patrol duties which continued into April.

Extensive operations had to await the arrival of more planes, procurement of suitable types of aircraft, training of personnel, and provision of necessary facilities. General Brereton's recent experience in the Philippines and Java made him keenly aware of certain needed improvements in materiel, tactics, and training. While many of his suggestions were adopted, other recommendations could not immediately receive favorable action. Requests for a more suitable type of fighter plane, for example, could not be met because such planes were not then available. Requests for P-38's equipped for photographic work met with the same answer.

As in the Southwest Pacific, the vast distances which had to be covered in reaching enemy targets precluded the use of fighter protection for bombers, forcing most operations to be carried out at night. This situation, combined with the lack of photographic aircraft and unfavorable atmospheric conditions, reduced the effectiveness of high-altitude precision bombing and pointed to medium bombers as more suitable for such operations. It was not until late in April, however, that arrangements were made for assigning 2 medium bombardment squadrons to the 7th Group, thereby changing the unit from a heavy bombardment to a composite group of 2 heavy and 2 medium squadrons.

Most of the aircraft arriving from the United States were in need of major repairs and, in some cases, complete overhaul before they could be put into combat. Many planes, including P-40's which were brought to the west African coast by the aircraft carrier Ranger, were damaged or wrecked in the flight across Africa. Upon reaching Karachi, those in need of engine replacement were sometimes forced to wait weeks before spares arrived. Extreme dust conditions also increased the demand for engine replacements.

The inactivity resulting from the lack of proper equipment for operational and training activities naturally affected the morale of airmen at Karachi. Moreover, throughout March the Japanese push through Burma and enemy activity in the Indian Ocean became so critical that attacks were expected even at Karachi. Almost equally depressing was the absence of mail from the United States. These factors, along with the unsatisfactory climate and the absence of recreational facilities, forced the men to lead a cheerless and monotonous existence.

It was not until early in April that the monotony could be broken, at least for part of the Tenth Air Force, by the beginning of bombing operations. On the night of 2/3 April a flight of 2 B-17's and 1 LB-30, manned by crews of the 9th Squadron and led by General Brereton, carried out a successful mission against enemy shipping near Port Blair in the Andaman Islands. Eight tons of bombs were dropped from 3,500 feet, scoring hits on a cruiser and a transport, both of which were left burning. The bombers encountered enemy fighters and intense antiaircraft fire but succeeded in returning to base with 2 of the planes damaged. A simultaneous attack by 2 B-17's was scheduled for targets in the Rangoon area, but 1 of the planes crashed on the take-off, killing the entire crew, and the other developed mechanical trouble. These operations entailed the use of an advanced base near Calcutta, a distance of approximately 1,200 air miles from Karachi. Subsequent operations were characterized by the same difficulties of distance and shortage of aircraft, as well as by unfavorable weather conditions. Such bombing raids therefore could be considered little more than harassing operations.

Improvement of the situation in the Indian Ocean, with British occupation of Madagascar and withdrawal of heavy units of the Japanese fleet toward the Pacific, brought clarification of the air force's primary mission. By the latter part of May, plans had been made to concentrate on aid to China. Induction of AVG personnel into the AAF had already been favorably considered in Washington, and in April Chennault was recalled to duty and promoted to brigadier general. The 23d Pursuit Group, which had been selected to absorb the AVG, was in process of moving through India to China, though not until 4 July was the change finally effected.

The India-China Ferry

In ferrying operations, the Tenth Air Force made its principal contribution to the early Allied effort in the CBI theater. Shortages of personnel and equipment and a lack of suitable fields and protective facilities did not prevent the 1st Ferrying Group from transporting supplies into Burma and China and evacuating wounded soldiers and civilian refugees while the Japanese were closing in upon important bases along the route. Original plans for the ferry called for two commands, the Trans-India, to operate from Karachi to Dinjan in Assam, and the Assam-Burma-China, to operate from Dinjan to Kunming. Plans for transferring cargo from one plane to another at Dinjan soon had to be abandoned because of the shortage of aircraft, and the idea of maintaining two separate commands was supplanted by the more practical one of an India-China Ferry.

For several months, however, the Assam-Burma-China Ferry, under the command of Col. Caleb V. Haynes, continued to retain its identity. This route naturally received immediate attention because of the necessity of transporting supplies to the Chinese, whose morale had suffered since the fall of Rangoon. Ten Pan American DC-3's from Africa were made available to the command, whose first task early in April was to deliver 30,000 gallons of gasoline and 500 gallons of oil to Chinese airfields for use by 16 B-25's which were then moving across the Pacific aboard an aircraft carrier preparatory to executing a daring attack on the Japanese homeland.

Immediately following the completion of this assignment, the transport planes were given a much larger task. When the Japanese push through Burma threatened to put the British and Chinese defenders to rout, the DC-3's carried ammunition and supplies into the battle area and evacuated refugees and wounded personnel. After the fall of Mandalay on 1 May the pilots defied every normal limit of load and altitude in order to evacuate as many passengers as possible before the Japanese could close in upon points on the ferry route to China. The planes were completely unarmed and subject to enemy attack, but not one transport was lost in these operations.

Ferry pilots and crews at Dinjan were normally under a constant strain, since the susceptibility to Japanese attack forced them to get the planes off the field at dawn. But during these operations into Burma the pilots were more than overworked. Even after the fall of Myitkyina on 8 May, they continued to drop food and supplies to the retreating defenders, including General Stilwell, who elected to "walk out" rather than be evacuated.

The loss of Burma called for a considerable amount of revision in plans for both ground and air operations. The ferry route to China, for example, could no longer be regarded merely as a supplement to regular supply lines; the new situation demanded an air cargo service large enough to replace the Burma Road. In this connection the ferry operations throughout April, May, and June had not only an intrinsic value, but a far-reaching effect as well, for their success pointed the way to the more ambitious undertaking of "over the hump" service, a later development which involved flying over the 18,000-foot Himalayas. Momentarily, however, flights from Dinjan to China were halted by the loss of bases in Burma and by the heavy rains of the monsoon season.

Supply and Maintenance

During the Burma operations a few reinforcements for the Tenth Air Force were arriving at Karachi and initial work was accomplished on the establishment of ground services essential to air combat. On 1 May the X Air Force Service Command was activated under Brig. Gen. Elmer E. Adler, who had arrived 5 days earlier from the Middle East. Necessary cadres were taken from other units of the Tenth Air Force; and Agra, approximately 700 miles east of Karachi, was selected as the most desirable location for the main depot.

Later in the month the 3d Air Depot Group arrived at Karachi, after a 60-day voyage from the United States, along with the ground echelon of the 23d Pursuit Group, additional personnel of the 1st Ferrying Group, and Headquarters and Headquarters Squadron, Tenth Air Force. On 28 May, with the arrival of the 3d Group at Agra, the 3d Air Depot was established. The immediate task was construction of barracks and an airdrome, in which native workers assisted. To provide "front-line" service to combat units, the 59th Materiel Squadron was divided into small base units and located at Allahabad, Kunming, Agra, Dinjan-Chabua, Chakulia, and at Bangalore, where an aircraft manufacturing plant was being converted into a repair and overhaul depot.

Bombardment Operations

While these services were being set up, the striking arm of the Tenth Air Force--though limited to a mere handful of heavy bombers--continued to hit at the enemy throughout Burma. Using advance bases at Asansol and Dum Dum, the planes bombed Rangoon shipping and air facilities as frequently as the condition of the aircraft would allow. Typical of the interruptions occurring during these early months, was the 2-week period following 3 April when operations had to be suspended while repairs were being made.

After the fall of the ferry base at Myitkyina on 8 May, the bombers divided their attention between this strategic point and the equally important targets at Rangoon, with four B-17's of the 9th Squadron making the first attack on Myitkyina on 12 May. Only by rendering this field unserviceable could the bombers protect the ferry route, for Japanese planes operating from this point could easily reach Dinjan and could also patrol the route to Kunming.

By mid-June all heavy bombers were grounded by the monsoon season and by a shortage of spare parts. The adverse weather, on the other hand, offered some respite from enemy operations and provided an opportunity for improvement of air-warning and antiaircraft facilities in the Assam and Calcutta areas. Strengthening of the Allied position in the Indian Ocean had already allowed the movement of units from Karachi eastward. The 436th Bombardment Squadron (redesignated from the 88th Reconnaissance Squadron) by the first part of June was moving to Allahabad, where the 9th Bombardment Squadron had preceded it on 27 April. Headquarters of the 7th Bombardment Group moved to Barrackpore, near Calcutta. The 51st Fighter Group was moving units into Kunming and Dinjan, while the 23d Fighter Group and the 11th Bombardment

Squadron (H) were assembling in China.

By June, the outlook for the Tenth Air Force was considerably brighter than it had been at any time during its existence. Important decisions had been rendered on the mission of the air force, on relations between the air force and the theater commander, and on the disposition of forces in China. Both ferry and service organizations had begun operations, while progress was evident in the provision of combat units with personnel and equipment. But, like the other Army air forces opposing the Japanese, the Tenth was still on the defensive; and enemy capabilities indicated still further advances in the China-Burma-India theater. Moreover, within the month, the Tenth Air Force was destined to lose virtually its entire striking arm when the British suffered a major defeat at Knightsbridge, and in the emergency General Brereton was ordered to the Middle East with all available bombers.

-VII-
THE TOKYO RAID

When transport crews of the Tenth Air Force ferried gasoline and oil to Chinese airfields early in April, they were making preparations for what proved to be the most spectacular combat undertaking of the AAF during the first half of 1942. The plan for bombing the Japanese homeland was first conceived in January, and preparations in the United States were carried out with utmost secrecy under the direction of Lt. Col. James H. Doolittle. Tests were conducted off Norfolk, Va., to determine the practicability of operating B-25's from the deck of an aircraft carrier. Volunteers from the 17th Bombardment Group made up the 24 crews which were ordered to Eglin Field, Fla., for special training. Not informed of their final destination, they knew only that they had volunteered for a hazardous but important mission.

At Eglin Field the tactical training of the crews was compressed into less than 1 month. A naval aviator was assigned to teach pilots the technique of lifting planes off the deck of a carrier. Practice take-offs were made on an auxiliary field near Eglin, with white lines drawn on the runways to represent the deck of a carrier. The pilots had no opportunity for a practice run from an actual deck. A limited amount of gunnery and bombing training was given, but much time was lost while armament personnel put the turrets in working order. The B-25's had been modified by the installation of 3 extra gas tanks-- 1 in the bomb bay, another in the space normally filled by the lower turret, and the third (a collapsible rubber bag) in the crawlway. To discourage attacks from the rear, 2 wooden .50-cal. guns were extended from the tip of the tail.

When it was found impossible to include all 24 planes on the mission, 16 planes and extra crews were ordered to Alameda (Calif.) Air Station. On the morning of 1 April the 16 B-25's were hoisted by giant cranes on to the deck of the aircraft carrier Hornet. With 71 officers and 130 enlisted men of the AAF aboard, the Hornet put out to sea. Training of the crews continued, and the flyers were finally told their objective. Specific military targets were assigned to each crew and minute details were discussed, with almost every eventuality taken into consideration.

On 13 April the Hornet made a rendevous with another task force, the combined forces now totaling 2 carriers (the Hornet and Enterprise), 1 light cruiser, 3 heavy cruisers, 8 destroyers, and 2 oilers. Maintaining radio silence, the force sailed westward under the command of Vice Adm. William F. Halsey, Jr. Plans called for the force to proceed to a point 400 miles from Tokyo. Colonel Doolittle was to take off 3 hours before the other planes in order to light up Tokyo with an incendiary attack early in the evening. The fires would guide 12 more B-25's which were to bomb the city with 9 tons of high explosives. The 3 remaining planes were to attack the cities of Nagoya, Kobe, and Osaka with incendiaries. The planes would then have just enough fuel to reach Chinese airfields where gasoline and flare pots had been assembled in anticipation of their arrival on the night of 19/20 April.

Events on the morning of 18 April prevented the 16 planes from carrying out original plans in their entirety. Having avoided 2 enemy surface craft, the task force sighted 2 more enemy vessels while still approximately 800 miles from Tokyo. One enemy patrol vessel was sunk, but it was feared that Japanese crewmen had already radioed a warning of the approaching force. The decision was made to launch the B-25's immediately. When Colonel Doolittle took off shortly after 0800, hours ahead of the scheduled time, the Hornet was 620 miles from the nearest point of Japanese land. None of the crews had any assurance that they would be able to reach the Chinese airfields, but they were at least sure that their targets were within range.

The planes did reach the targets, and the Japanese people were apparently taken completely by surprise. The B-25's flew in at a minimum altitude, skimming the waves until they reached the coastline and then flying as low as the rugged terrain would permit. Groups of villagers, thinking the planes were Japanese, waved to them on their way as they passed overhead. The first bombs were dropped on Tokyo at 1215. By the time the last bombers flew in, the city had been alerted and the aircraft met fairly heavy concentrations of fire. Military targets were hit in Tokyo, Nagoya, Yokosuka, Kobe, and Yokohama. Only one B-25 was forced to jettison its bombs, and not one plane was lost as a result of enemy action.

A fierce storm, growing darkness, and dwindling fuel supplies combined to bring about the loss of all the B-25's after they had completed the bombing. Most of the planes reached the China coast and came down in nearby waters or on treacherous mountainsides. One plane landed in Russia, where its crew was interned. Two other crews fell into Japanese hands, and some of these airmen were executed. With one exception, crews of the other planes escaped with their lives, though many were injured. The material loss to the AAF was considerable, but at the time the effect was regarded as well worth the expenditure of 16 medium bombers. For the Americans, it was the one bright spot in the whole somber picture of early 1942. But, like the 12 and 13 April bombardment of the Philippines, it was only a token action and could not be repeated any time in the immediate future.

THE ALLIED AIR FORCES--CORAL SEA

With the approach of May 1942, the Pacific war entered an especially critical phase for the Allies. The month of April had been marked by a noticeable lack of enemy activity--a lull which seemed to presage renewed Japanese efforts. The situation demanded the utmost alertness on the part of Allied forces, for the enemy was capable of striking in any one of several directions or in several areas simultaneously. A major attack might be made in the Southwest Pacific against the Australian continent, New Guinea, or the Solomons; or in the Central Pacific against Midway or Hawaii; or in the North Pacific against the Aleutians. Before the passing of 2 more months the Japanese struck in all three areas. And when the crisis came, American air and naval power proved to be sufficient.

The first attempt was made in the Southwest Pacific. On 4 May a sizable enemy force moved into the port of Tulagi in the southeastern Solomons, although Allied aircraft attacked the vessels and sank a light cruiser, 2 destroyers, 4 gunboats, and a supply craft. Having secured their flank position as a preliminary step toward a larger operation, the Japanese began their next move westward through the Coral Sea. Land-based aircraft operating out of Australia on 6 May first discovered units of the enemy fleet moving in 7 groups and totaling 2 aircraft carriers, 7 cruisers, 17 destroyers, 16 unidentified warships, 2 submarines, 1 submarine tender, and 21 transport ships.

On the basis of information furnished by the American reconnaissance planes, Allied naval forces moved into the area and on 7 and 8 May were attacked by enemy planes in the vicinity of the Louisiade Archipelago. While 23 Japanese planes were being shot down in this area, Allied carrier-based planes and all the aircraft which could be assembled on the northeast coast of Australia were engaged in bombing the main units of the Japanese fleet. On 9 May enemy ships which could still maneuver after the attacks were observed withdrawing to the north.

Action throughout the engagement was confined to contact between the Japanese and Allied air forces and between air and naval forces; there was no contact between the opposing surface units. It was carrier- and land-based aircraft alone which succeeded in routing the invasion fleet and in sinking 1 aircraft carrier, 1 heavy cruiser, 2 light cruisers, 2 destroyers, 4 gunboats, 2 transports, and 1 submarine. In addition, more than 100 enemy aircraft were destroyed, and another aircraft carrier, light cruiser, transport, and submarine were damaged. American losses included the aircraft carrier Lexington, 1 destroyer, 1 tanker, and 66 planes.

The 3d, 19th, and 22d Bombardment Groups, and several fighter squadrons of the Allied Air Forces in Australia participated in the action and continued to attack the withdrawing enemy vessels until they were out of range. They also carried out reconnaissance and patrol missions throughout the engagement. For the most part there was effective coordination between the Allied Air Forces and the naval forces, but some of the airmen—having been furnished no information as to the position of American naval units—unwittingly bombed certain of those units. The situation was to improve with the passing of time and with the growth of Army and Navy forces, for it was only by a high degree of coördination that the Allies were able to launch and successfully execute their first offensive in this section of the Pacific. Until the late summer of 1942 these forces were still on the defensive, but the Coral Sea action was significant as the first major defeat of the Japanese and, therefore, as a turning point in the Pacific war.

I. THE SEVENTH AIR FORCE—MIDWAY

After their defeat in the Coral Sea, the Japanese began to withdraw many of their vessels from the Southwest Pacific toward Japan and to assemble forces for a large-scale offensive. Since there were no indications of the exact direction in which the next invasion attempt would be made, American military and naval units throughout the Pacific Ocean and along the coast from Alaska to Panama took special precautionary measures and reinforced their garrisons. Predictions and conjectures as to Japanese intentions were no longer necessary after 3 June, for an enemy fleet of approximately 80 vessels was then discovered moving toward Midway. The ensuing air and naval battle, a series of complex actions spread over 3 days and nights, with Army, Navy, and Marine Corps units cooperating, resulted in an even greater defeat for the Japanese than did the Coral Sea engagement.

The Battle of Midway gave the Seventh Air Force its first real opportunity to meet the Japanese since 7 December 1941. A number of changes had taken place in the air force after the attack on Pearl Harbor. On 18 December Maj. Gen. Clarence L. Tinker succeeded Maj. Gen. Frederick L. Martin as commander of the Hawaiian Air Force. Tactical and administrative functions increased as the air units widened the scope of their activities. To meet the new demands of service and supply, the Hawaiian Air Force Base Command was established at Hickam Field on 25 December and was charged with control of all air base commands and depots.

Other changes in early 1942 had affected the designation but not necessarily the function of the various components. The Hawaiian Air Force became the Seventh Air Force on 5 February; and by subsequent action the Base Command became the VII Air Force Base Command, the 18th Bombardment Wing became the VII Bomber Command, and the Hawaiian Interceptor Command (redesignated from the 14th Pursuit Wing) became the VII Fighter Command.

Activities of these units throughout the first half of 1942 were centered around defense of the islands and assimilation of new personnel, aircraft, and equipment. The VII Fighter Command was able to engage in an intensive training program, and at the same time was carrying out a few antisubmarine patrol and convoy duties. The VII Bomber Command, on the other hand, could devote little time to training functions, for until 1 April all bombers were assigned to reconnaissance or striking forces. At the beginning of April approximately 25 per cent of the bombers were made available for a limited amount of training daily. In all its constant patrol and numerous submarine search missions, however, the Seventh Air Force had little chance to contact enemy forces. From 7 December 1941 to 1 March 1942, only 10 submarines had been attacked, 3 of which were probably sunk. In comparison with the Southwest Pacific, the Central Pacific had been a relatively inactive theater of war.

Definite signs of more activity in this area were seen on 18 May, when the Seventh Air Force was placed on a special alert to meet a threatened enemy attack. At that time 34 B-17's were on hand, of which 27 were suitable for combat. For 10 days no B-17's were used on search missions but were held in readiness as a striking force--completely fueled and loaded with 500- and 600-pound demolition bombs. From 18 May to 10 June a total of 60 B-17's arrived from the United States and were made available to tactical units after only 24 hours' maintenance and servicing.

In line with the principle of unity of command, all Seventh Air Force bombers were placed under operational control of the Navy; and after almost 2 weeks of alert, one squadron of 6 B-17's was ordered by Patrol Wing Two to fly to Midway. Following its arrival on 30 May the squadron flew two 800-mile search missions on the next 2 days. Similar missions were flown on the same days by another squadron of 6 B-17's which had been ordered from Oahu to Midway on 31 May. In the absence of ground crews, combat personnel had to perform their own maintenance at Midway.

When on the morning of 3 June naval patrol planes sighted a large concentration of eastward bound enemy vessels about 700 miles from Midway, the B-17 crews had already flown approximately 30 hours within 2 days. Six additional bombers were sent from Oahu, and at 1623, 9 B-17's were ordered to attack the enemy force, now reported only 570 miles off Midway and approaching in 5 columns. Attacking from 8,000 feet with 36 x 600-pound bombs, the B-17's scored a total of 5 hits and 5 near misses on 2 battleships or heavy cruisers and 2 large transports, leaving 1 warship and 1 transport burning and severely damaged. During the night 4 Catalinas attacked the same group and scored 2 torpedo hits, one of which was believed to have sunk an enemy ship.

For the next 3 days Army, Navy, and Marine Corps planes took off from Midway, Oahu, and from carriers which had been brought into position, the complexity of the action making it difficult to give an accurate account of the damage inflicted by any one group. While these forces were pounding the enemy vessels with bombs and torpedoes on the morning of 4 June, enemy carrier-based planes attacked Midway. An outnumbered Marine fighter force met the approaching planes and, in conjunction with antiaircraft batteries, shot down 40 Japanese aircraft. Since the enemy force was now only 180 miles from Midway, 4 B-26's armed with torpedoes were thrown into the attack. They met heavy fighter opposition and antiaircraft fire, and 2 of the B-26's were shot down. The remaining 2 planes scored hits and then returned to Midway, where they were forced to crash-land.

By sundown of 4 June, American forces had gained control of the air in the vicinity of Midway. Two enemy carriers had been hit so many times that they sank or were sunk by the Japanese before the following morning. One enemy destroyer had been sunk, and 2 battleships, 1 transport, and several other ships had been damaged. The U. S. carrier <u>Yorktown</u>, put out of action by enemy aircraft, would probably have survived; but a submarine attack on the next day resulted in further damage and the carrier had to be sunk by attending forces.

By early morning of 5 June the enemy force had separated into several groups, all in full retreat. Throughout the morning and afternoon B-17's from Midway sought out the fleeing vessels and claimed a number of hits on enemy warships, although unfavorable weather made the missions extremely hazardous. During the night U. S. aircraft carriers steamed westward in pursuit of the Japanese. Early the next morning, 6 June, carrier aircraft discovered 2 groups of enemy warships, and attacks were made on the ships from approximately 0930 to 1730. Twelve additional B-17's were ordered from Oahu to Midway.

After 6 June, repeated efforts were made to contact the remainder of the enemy fleet, but without success. Except for mopping-up activities and search missions, the Battle of Midway was ended. On 9 June, while a flight of B-17's was continuing the search, a plane carrying Maj. Gen. Clarence L. Tinker was forced down at sea and lost. Command of the Seventh Air Force was then assumed by Brig. Gen. H. C. Davidson.

During the 3-day engagement the combined Army, Navy, and Marine Corps air units sank 4 Japanese aircraft carriers, 2 heavy cruisers, 3 destroyers, and 1 or more transports or auxiliary vessels. Damage was inflicted on 3 enemy battleships, 3 heavy cruisers, 1 light cruiser, several destroyers, and at least 3 auxiliary ships. Approximately 275 Japanese aircraft were destroyed or lost from lack of flight decks for landing. An estimated 4,800 Japanese were killed.

U. S. naval losses included the carrier Yorktown and the destroyer Hammann. Approximately 150 naval planes were lost in action or damaged beyond repair. Personnel losses were 92 officers and 215 enlisted men.

Participation by AAF units became much larger than was expected, because of the early location of enemy carriers. For most of the personnel the Battle of Midway was their first combat action. Besides the handicap of inexperience, the crews in some cases had to contend with mechanical difficulties in their planes—difficulties which could undoubtedly have been eliminated if the situation had allowed for proper testing before sending the bombers into action. A further strain was placed on combat crews at Midway by the absence of sufficient ground crews. Even under these conditions, the B-17's flew a total of 55 missions during the 3 days of the battle. They bombed a total of 7 battleships or heavy cruisers, 7 carriers, 1 destroyer, and 2 transports, resulting in claims of 22 direct hits, 6 probable hits, and 46 near misses. Ten out of 18 enemy fighters encountered were shot down and 2 were damaged. Two B-17's and 2 B-26's were lost at sea and 2 more of each type were damaged.

Units of the Seventh Air Force which participated in the engagement included the 26th, 42d, and 431st Squadrons of the 11th Bombardment Group, and the 23d, 31st, and 72d Squadrons of the 5th Bombardment Group. The 72d Squadron had been equipped with B-18's until more B-17's began to arrive from the United States in May. Since the unit was not fully equipped until 2 days before being committed to combat, there was of course no opportunity for proper training of the crews.

Other B-17's were flown by the 1st Provisional Squadron, which was en route from the United States to the Fiji Islands. Two of the B-26's were assigned to the 69th Bombardment Squadron, also en route to the Fijis, and the remaining 2 B-26's were en route to Australia as reinforcements for the 408th Squadron of the 22d Bombardment Group. Units of the VII Fighter Command took no active part in the Battle of Midway, but the 73d Squadron of the 18th Fighter Group almost immediately thereafter was sent to become a part of the Midway defense forces, replacing an almost-decimated Marine fighter unit.

The Midway engagement provided some valuable combat lessons, many of them already known but now given fresh emphasis. As in the Coral Sea action, maximum results could not be achieved without a sufficient number of planes over the target at one time. Army medium bombers proved to be effective torpedo aircraft; but without simultaneous attacks by other types of planes to disperse enemy fire, torpedo attacks were tantamount to suicide. For example, out of one group of 15 Navy torpedo planes which attacked an enemy carrier, not one returned. Japanese fighter aircraft were still superior to American fighter planes at high altitudes, but the Japanese pilots again demonstrated their hesitancy in attacking B-17's in close formation. Above all, the Battle of Midway proved that heavy bombers of the Seventh Air Force were not doomed to a relatively immobile life around Oahu but that they could be used effectively in cooperation with the fleet and in defense of outlying bases. As a further demonstration of their mobility, just 2 weeks after the Midway battle, 3 LB-30's of the Seventh

Air Force struck at the enemy in a night bombing attack on Wake Island, involving a flight of almost 2,500 miles from Oahu.

In one respect the Battle of Midway represented a decided advance over the Coral Sea action, for the principle of unity of command was followed and proved to be sound. All American forces fought under Adm. Chester W. Nimitz, Commander in Chief of the Pacific Fleet, with other Navy, Marine Corps, and Army officers occupying subordinate commands. While operational conditions were not entirely satisfactory, they allowed the combined forces to marshal sufficient strength for rendering the Japanese Navy its second great defeat of the war. As in the Coral Sea battle just 1 month before, there was no contact between surface units of the opposing forces; it was another triumph for air power. Midway, which might have become a Japanese steppingstone to Pacific Fleet headquarters in Hawaii and eventually to the western coast of the United States, was still held by American forces as a steppingstone to Japanese-occupied islands in the Central Pacific.

THE ELEVENTH AIR FORCE—DUTCH HARBOR

The Japanese thrust at Midway was only one part of a two-pronged invasion attempt. While approximately 80 vessels were moving toward Midway, another large enemy force was headed for American bases in the Aleutians—that string of islands jutting out from Alaska toward Japan's Kurile Islands and Russia's Kamchatka Peninsula. On 18 May, the same day that forces in Hawaii were alerted, naval intelligence received word that Japanese amphibious forces were preparing for an attack on Alaska which would probably materialize during the first 3 days of June. The invasion force was reported to consist of approximately 2 aircraft carriers, 5 cruisers, 12 destroyers, 8 submarines, 2 or 3 seaplane tenders, and a number of transports, cargo vessels, and heavy bombers.

Maneuvering under cover of bad weather, the enemy neared Unalaska Island, location of the important naval base of Dutch Harbor, and on 3 June attacked both the harbor and Army installations at Fort Mears. A strafing sweep by fighter planes over the naval air station was followed by four flights of bombers, composed of 3 or 4 planes each, which bombed the Fort Mears area. Shortly after this preliminary sweep the Japanese discovered that they had not caught American forces unprepared. Instead of having to defend Dutch Harbor from bases 1,000 miles eastward, the Eleventh Air Force operated planes from bases which had been secretly prepared at Umnak and Cold Bay on either side of Unalaska. After 18 May, aerial reinforcements were rushed from the mainland just as they were sent to Oahu to meet the enemy threat in that area, but it was primarily the existence of these airfields in the Aleutians which enabled the Eleventh Air Force to interfere with enemy plans.

During the previous 5 months, the air force had been busy with an extensive airfield construction program and with other preparations. Though the outbreak of war had resulted in a hurried call for reinforcements, only 2 additional squadrons could be sent from the United States. Early in January 1942 the 77th Bombardment Squadron (M) and the 11th Pursuit Squadron were moved to Elmendorf. Organizational steps were taken to increase the effectiveness of the air force. After being redesignated as the Alaskan Air Force on 10 January, it was given a numerical designation on 5 February when it became the Eleventh Air Force. It comprised a Headquarters and Headquarters Squadron; the Provisional Interceptor Command, Alaska, commanded by Maj. Norman D. Sillin and composed of the 11th and 18th Pursuit Squadrons; the 28th Composite Group, commanded by Maj. William O. Eareckson and composed of the 73d and 77th Bombardment Squadrons (M) and the 36th Bombardment Squadron (H); and the 23d Air Base Group which, along with the sub-depot at Elmendorf, supplied maintenance service for tactical units. The small air force, composed of only 2,960 officers and men, was headed by Brig. Gen. William O. Butler, who assumed command on 8 March 1942. Shortages of planes and pilots were keenly felt when long periods of daylight necessitated keeping patrols in the air for 14 or more hours.

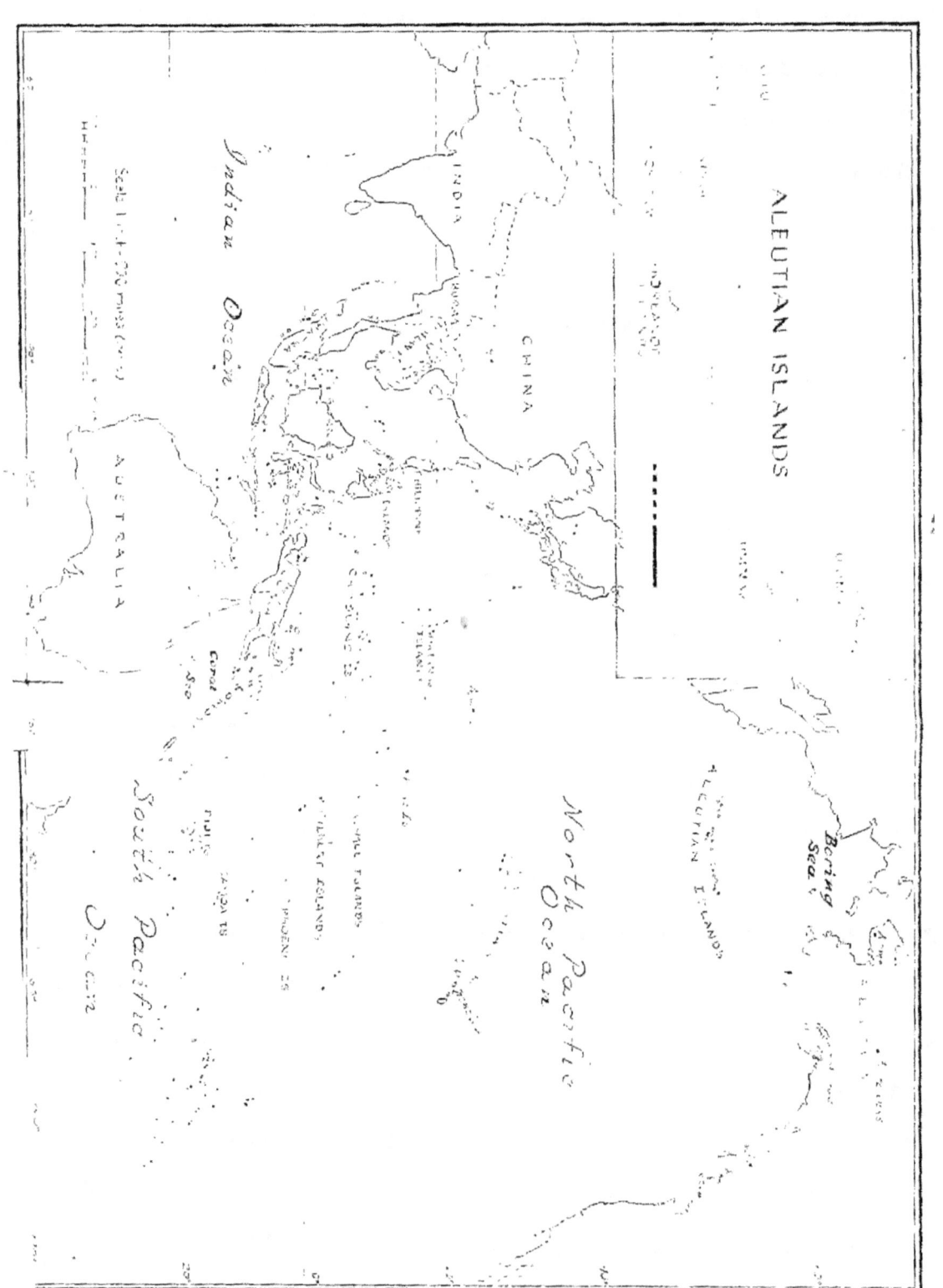

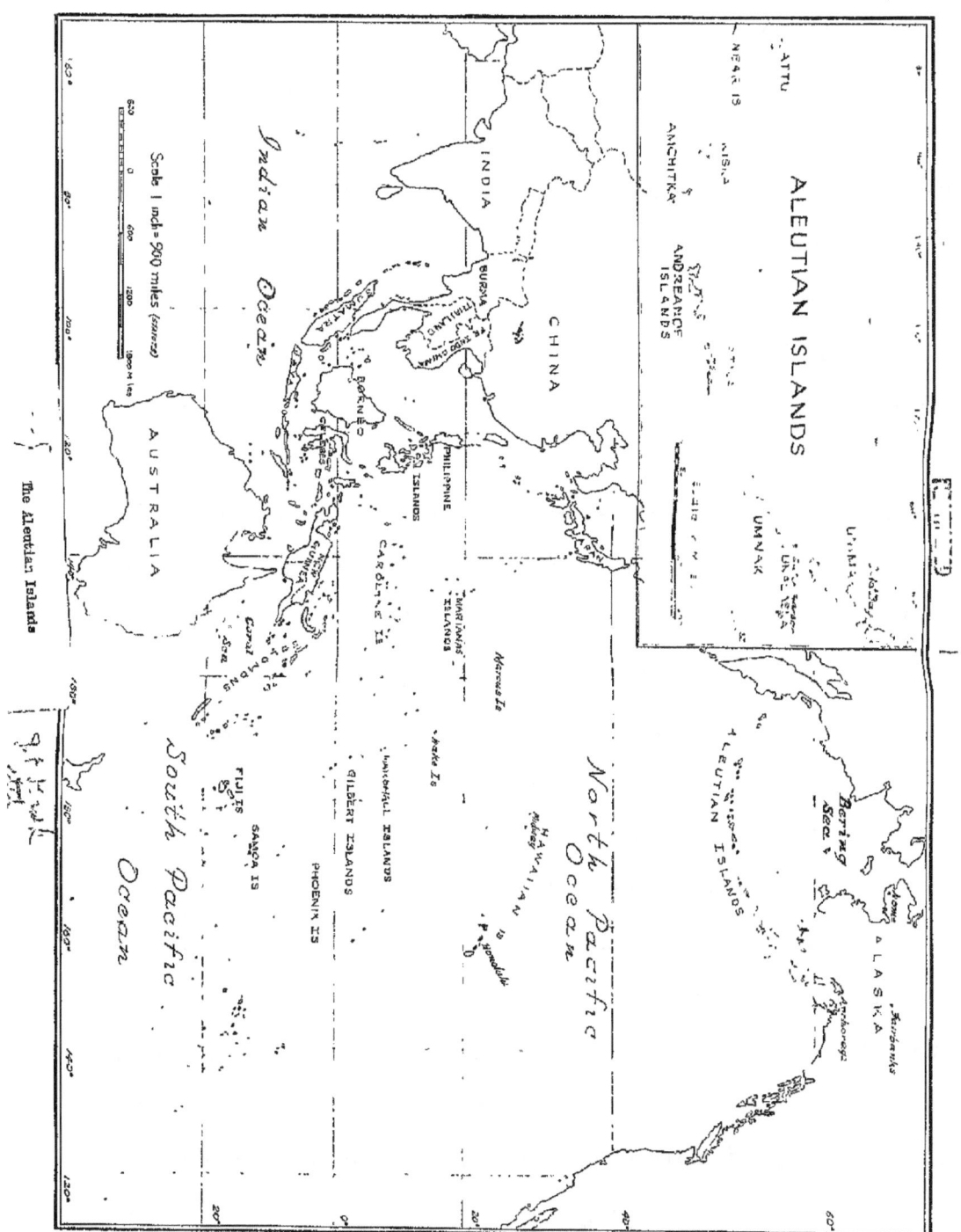

The Aleutian Islands

Since April, May, and June were the best months for flying—and consequently the most likely time of enemy attack—the Eleventh Air Force throughout the winter and spring of 1942 raced against time and the Alaskan weather. The first of the tactical units to move from Elmendorf, the 36th Bombardment Squadron, on 1 February shifted southward to Fort Greely on Kodiak Island. Further moves toward the Aleutian chain had to await additional work on airfields at Naknek, Fort Randall (Cold Bay), and Fort Glenn (Umnak). Arctic and sub-arctic conditions were hardly conducive to speedy construction of the fields, while the transportation of supplies and personnel from the West Coast of the United States was necessarily slow. It was possible to work in temperatures as low as 50° below zero, but only by thawing practically all tools and materials before using them. Furthermore, construction of hard-surfaced runways could not be undertaken without the removal of muskeg, a spongy mass of accumulated roots and moss varying from several inches to several feet deep.

By early spring of 1942 there were approximately eight fields in Alaska capable of use by combat aircraft, but the important fields in the Aleutians were not among them. Work still continued on these and other projects, and by the middle of May, 5,000-foot runways of steel matting had been completed at Cold Bay and Umnak, though revetments, parking and dispersal areas, essential supplies and equipment for operations, and an adequate warning system had not been provided.

Dutch Harbor

When word was received on 18 May of an impending Japanese attack, the Eleventh Air Force acted swiftly. Navy planes operating from Kodiak and Sitka and Army planes operating from Kodiak and Elmendorf would be of little use in stopping the Japanese if they attempted to invade the Aleutians. It was clear that Army planes must be moved to the partially completed fields in the Aleutians. Every available boat and transport plane—military and commercial—was commandeered to take supplies to the airfields, while combat units prepared to move in and additional units were shifted from the West Coast to Alaska. The 36th Bombardment Squadron at Kodiak was reinforced by 6 B-17's; and the 54th Fighter Squadron, with new P-38's, was sent via water and air transport from Seattle to Elmendorf. By 2 June part of the 73d and 77th Bombardment Squadrons and the 11th Fighter Squadron had moved to Cold Bay and Umnak, 6 B-26's and 16 P-40's being concentrated at the former field and 6 B-26's and 17 P-40's at the latter. Advance headquarters for the Eleventh Air Force had been established at Kodiak, and all Army and Navy forces—now operating under Rear Adm. R. A. Theobald of U. S. Navy Task Force 8—awaited the Japanese attack.

Constant patrols had been maintained by Catalinas and the one B-17E which the 36th Squadron had prior to reinforcement. On 2 June a Catalina spotted the enemy fleet through a break in the overcast but contact was soon lost. On the following day the B-17 searched all the way to Kiska for some sign of the enemy force. Nothing was seen except a dense fog along the island chain. Safely concealed behind a weather front, the Japanese moved in toward Dutch Harbor. The initial attack on 3 June, made in relatively small force by carrier-based aircraft, was apparently designed for reconnaissance purposes as much as for any other.

The only contact made between the Eleventh Air Force and the Japanese on 3 June occurred when a P-40 shot down an enemy float plane which appeared over Otter Point, where the Umnak airfield was located. Until this time the existence of Army air facilities in the Aleutians had been a well-kept secret—one of which the Japanese were not made fully aware until the following day.

While more reinforcements of B-17's and PBY's were flying from San Diego, Calif., air units already in Alaska were shifted toward the Aleutians for operations on 4 June. Rear defenses were also strengthened, when RCAF units stationed at Annette Island dispatched 1 squadron of Bolingbrokes to Yakutat for protection of that area. When Navy Patrol Wing Four reported enemy vessels about 160 miles southwest of Umnak early on the morning of 4 June, all available units of the Eleventh Air Force were ordered to attack. As the American crews made repeated sorties, a fog moved in to screen the enemy forces, with the result that only a few contacts were made. Several hits on vessels were reported, while 1 B-17 and 1 B-26 were lost.

During the afternoon the Japanese made a determined attack on Dutch Harbor with approximately 10 bombers and 16 fighters, causing a considerable amount of damage to warehouses and oil tanks. One flight of 8 enemy planes, while passing near Otter Point, was attacked by 8 P-40's of the 11th Squadron. In the ensuing engagement 4 Japanese planes were shot down at the expense of 2 P-40's and 1 pilot.

After 4 June the Japanese made no further concerted offensive efforts; instead they fell back to the outer Aleutians. During their withdrawal, enemy forces successfully eluded American patrols by taking cover behind a weather front. After 1 week, Navy patrols discovered the enemy on Attu and Kiska, and from that time forward the action of the Eleventh Air Force placed the Japanese on the defensive.

The numerous attack and search missions carried out by the Eleventh Air Force during the attempted enemy invasion of Dutch Harbor were performed under the most difficult operating conditions. The weather was marked by almost continuous rain and fog; ceilings ranged from zero to 500 feet, with visibility seldom more than 5 miles. Navigation was performed almost entirely by reckoning, while most of the flying was done just above the water's surface. Combat crews were kept under a continuous strain. In addition to performing most of their own aircraft maintenance work, the crews had to set up their own tents--in a sea of mud--and cook most of their own meals with practically no facilities. Both Cold Bay and Umnak were constantly subject to enemy attack, and crews were kept on the alert from dawn until dark, which at that time of year was from 0400 to 2300. Planes were refueled by gasoline pumped from barrels and by oil poured from five-gallon cans.

Army Air Action

Land-based air power, which had helped to stop the Japanese invasion attempt, was eventually to aid in driving the enemy out of the Aleutians; but at the moment no immediate action could be taken to recapture Kiska and Attu, since most of the available ships, planes, and trained troops were needed to maintain Allied positions in the Central, South, and Southwest Pacific.

After 6 months of war the Japanese had been stopped---at least temporarily---in the North, Central, and Southwest Pacific. By this time the American air forces throughout this vast area were able to maintain their positions, though only by a dangerously slim margin. Much progress had been made in providing the three elements necessary for successful aerial warfare---strategically located bases, trained personnel, and the proper aircraft and other equipment. But American forces did not possess the initiative in the war against Japan. Supply lines were still somewhat tenuous, shipping facilities from the United States were still over-taxed, and planes and men were still not available in adequate numbers. The Japanese, on the other hand, remained in control of a vast area throughout the Pacific, and there was no indication that they intended to stop with their present holdings.

I. GUADALCANAL AND ORIGINS OF THE THIRTEENTH AIR FORCE

Although American forces had won decisive victories during the crisis of May and June, the Coral Sea, Midway, and Dutch Harbor actions were essentially defensive victories. In Allied strategy the secondary position of the Japanese war did not allow for any full-scale offensive, but during the latter half of 1942 the war against Japan involved considerably more action than the term "strategic defensive" would strictly imply.

As early as April 1942 the Combined Chiefs of Staff had agreed that American forces should undertake a limited offensive in the South Pacific in order to prevent further Japanese encroachment upon the vital supply line to Australia. Mounting of the action had to await both the Navy's partial recovery from the blow at Pearl Harbor and the gradual assembly and organization of forces in the South Pacific. Finally, on 7 August, land, sea, and air forces launched the first American amphibious operation of the war by invading enemy-held territory in the lower Solomon Islands. Both initial operations and the more arduous task of holding the bases seized were largely the work of U. S. Navy and Marine forces. But certain units of the Army Air Forces, though small in number and not organized as a separate air force, participated in the entire action and shared with Marine and Naval forces the dangers and discomforts of Guadalcanal, the operational difficulties of the South Pacific, and the morale-corroding experience of fighting under primitive conditions.

Role of the Seventh Air Force

The Seventh Air Force, commanded after 20 June by Maj. Gen. Willis H. Hale, was called upon to provide a major portion of the Army air units for the Guadalcanal offensive, although the air force had barely enough tactical squadrons to carry out its own responsibilities in the Central Pacific. By the end of June the 73d Fighter Squadron was defending Midway, the 12th Fighter Squadron and a detachment of the 46th Squadron were at Christmas Island, while in September the newly-activated 333d Fighter Squadron began its defense of Canton Island. The bulk of the air force, still based on Oahu, was engaged in patrolling the Hawaiian Islands and in training and processing forces en route from the United States to the South and Southwest Pacific. These multiple duties left little opportunity for the Seventh Air Force to strike at the enemy in the Central Pacific. Except for an attack on Wake Island on 22 December, operations were limited to a few small-scale reconnaissance flights over Wake and the Gilbert Islands. The December raid, executed by 26 B-24D's of the 307th Bombardment Group, was the longest offensive mass flight attempted up to that time--a 5,000-mile mission staged through Midway.

Such attacks might have occurred more frequently if the offensive in the South Pacific had not claimed the only two experienced heavy bombardment groups of the Seventh Air Force. The ground echelon of the 11th Group left Oahu on 10 July, followed 1 week later by the air echelon with 35 B-17E's. In the latter part of September the first units of the 5th Bombardment Group began moving southward, and on 5 December the entire 5th and 11th Groups, the 12th and 44th Fighter Squadrons, and two service units were reassigned from the Seventh Air Force to the AAF in the South Pacific.

South Pacific Forces

Even before a move against the Solomons was decided upon, slender forces had been sent to garrison some of the island stepping-stones to Australia. In March, Army forces under the command of Brig. Gen. Alexander M. Patch reached New Caledonia after trans-shipping at Melbourne, Australia. Included in the shipment was the 67th Fighter Squadron, which had been augmented in Australia by 15 pilots. In less than a month after arriving at Noumea most of the squadron's 45 crated P-400's and 2 P-39F's were assembled on a half-completed airfield at Tontouta, though pilots and mechanics alike were hampered by almost total unfamiliarity with the aircraft type, by a woeful lack of tools, and by a superabundance of rain, mud, and mosquitoes. Training activities were conducted from three cow-pasture fields on the island, while 12 of the pilots made a 325-mile overwater flight to Efate for 3 weeks' gunnery instruction by Marine flyers.

The 67th Squadron's counterpart in the Fiji Islands was the 70th Fighter Squadron, which had arrived from the United States late in January. Medium bombardment strength in the Fijis consisted of the 70th Squadron of the 38th Group, whose ground echelon was dispatched

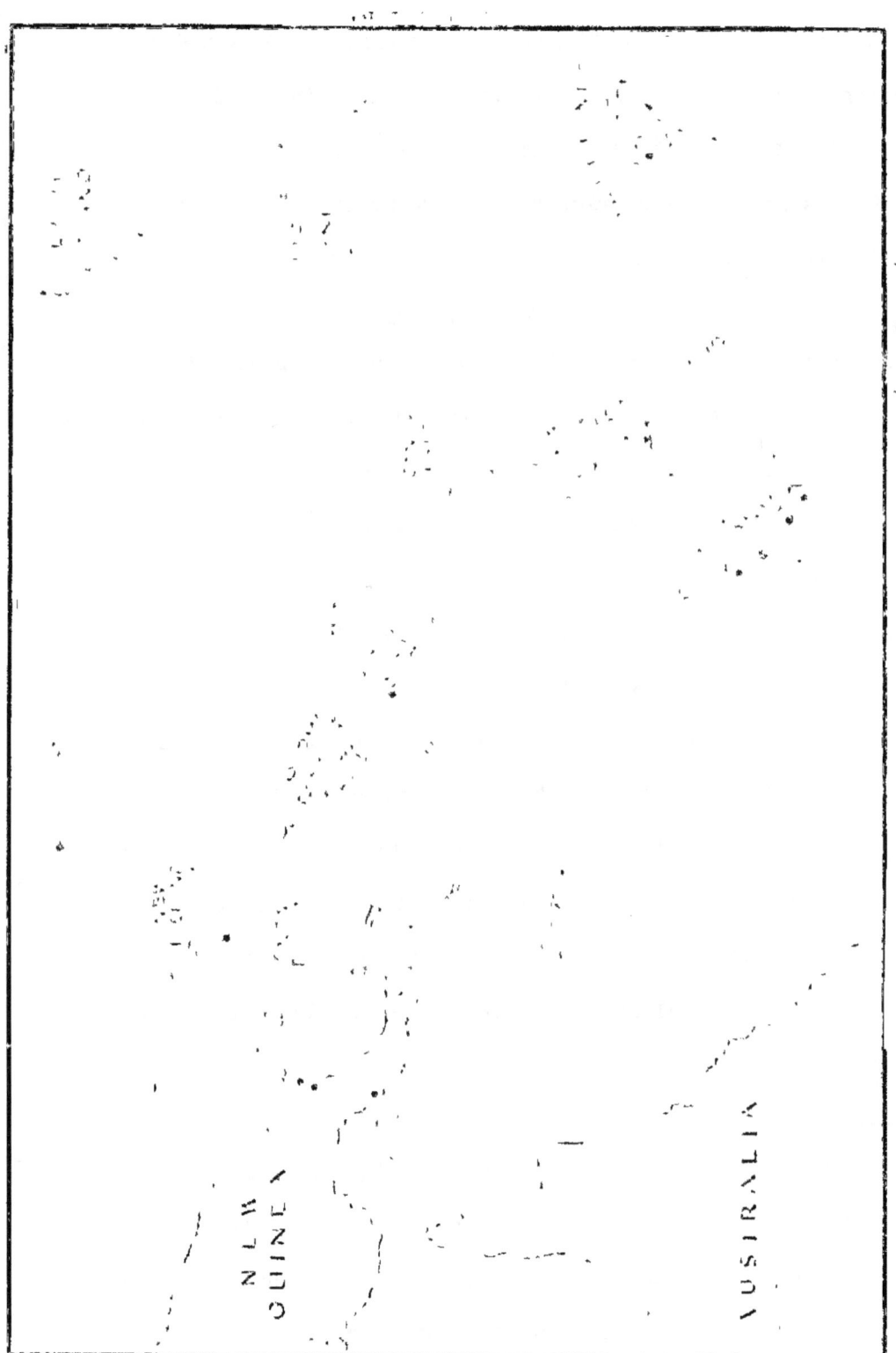

The Solomons and Related Areas

from Australia in May. The 69th Squadron of the same group was sent simultaneously to New Caledonia. The flying echelons, however, were just completing their training in the United States and were further delayed by orders holding them in Hawaii until after the Midway battle in June.

While Army, Navy, and Marine air units were taking up their stations in the South Pacific islands, important decisions were being made in Washington as to the ultimate strength necessary to hold the islands and the type of command and organization best suited to the theater. Long-range bombers and reconnaissance planes were essential needs of the area, yet AAF commitments to other theaters left no such planes for immediate assignment to the South Pacific. The immediate solution to the dilemma was found in designating the 11th Bombardment Group in Hawaii and the 19th Bombardment Group in Australia as mobile units, to be moved to any point along the island chain in case of an emergency.

All U. S. air, ground, and naval forces in the South Pacific Area and certain New Zealand units were placed under the command of Vice Adm. Robert L. Ghormley. One week before the opening of the Guadalcanal offensive, Maj. Gen. Millard F. Harmon arrived to assume command of U. S. Army forces in the area. His chief of staff was Brig. Gen. Nathan F. Twining, also an airman. In line with the principle of unity of command, however, the area commander retained operational control of all forces, and a naval commander under Admiral Ghormley controlled operations of all land-based aircraft.

Procedures were established for coordination of effort among the widely scattered bases and between bases and task forces at sea. The outline for both organizational and operational procedures received the approval of Admiral Ghormley and General Harmon on 4 August.

Preparations for the offensive had gone forward rapidly, as intelligence reports indicated an increasing Japanese activity in the lower Solomons. Since 4 May the enemy had been established at Tulagi on Florida Island. Early in June enemy troops went ashore on the Lunga Plain of Guadalcanal, just across the channel from Tulagi, and began construction of an airfield. Supported by numerous bases, airfields, and seaplane anchorages on Bougainville and other islands in the upper Solomons, the enemy was now getting into a position to strike southward from Guadalcanal against the New Hebrides or even New Caledonia. An immediate offensive against the Tulagi-Guadalcanal positions was imperative if American forces were to keep the line to Australia inviolate.

The First Marine Division, commanded by Maj. Gen. A. A. Vandegrift, was waiting in New Zealand. Surface craft began to assemble at Wellington, New Zealand, while aircraft were dispersed to new fields on New Caledonia, the New Hebrides, and the Fijis. Arrangements were made for General MacArthur's air forces in the Southwest Pacific to carry out reconnaissance and bombing missions against enemy bases in the Northern Solomons and Northeast New Guinea, in coordination with the Guadalcanal offensive. During the last week of July, B-17's of the

11th Bombardment Group, ordered from their base in Hawaii, began arriving in the South Pacific. Although ground crews were still at sea, the group began immediate search and photographic missions from Efate over the Tulagi-Guadalcanal-Gavutu area, using Marine photographers and Navy cameras--an arrangement which came to be standard until AAF photographic units could arrive in the following year.

Bomber Operations

For operations preliminary to the Marine landings, air units in the South Pacific were divided into 2 task groups. One force--centered on New Caledonia--was composed of 2 PBY's, the 69th Bombardment Squadron with 10 B-26's, the 67th Fighter Squadron with 38 P-400's, and New Zealand units with approximately 18 Hudsons. The 11th Group, under the command of Col. Laverne G. Saunders, made up the second force which, in addition to its reconnaissance activity, was ordered to hit Tulagi and Guadalcanal with maximum force from 31 July through 6 August. During this period the B-17's made 22 reconnaissance sorties and 56 bombing sorties, flying 710 nautical miles out from the field at Efate and, after the first of August, returning by way of a new field at Espiritu Santo.

Rabaul, key point in support of enemy operations in the Solomons and New Guinea, had been hit with increasing frequency since May by the 19th Bombardment Group from Australia; and even the 22d Bombardment Group had occasionally sent its B-26's against this distant target. A 19th Group attack of 7 August on Vunakanau airdrome at Rabaul was timed to coincide with the Marine invasion of Guadalcanal. Thirteen planes reached the target, where enemy fighters were waiting to intercept with head-on attacks. Seven Japanese planes were shot down, at a cost of 1 B-17. Reliable reports of bombing results indicated later that at least 50 enemy aircraft were destroyed on the ground, thereby greatly curtailing the air power which might have been thrown against the Marine landings. The 19th Group, with rarely more than 20 B-17's in commission at any one time, continued to support the Solomons operations with reconnaissance and bombing missions. RAAF Hudsons and PBY's provided some assistance, while the heavy bombers concentrated on neutralization of such enemy bases as Kieta and Buka in the Solomons, in addition to Rabaul.

Invasion forces moved in upon Guadalcanal and Tulagi early on the morning of 7 August, supported by a heavy shore bombardment from fleet units. At Guadalcanal enemy troops took to the hills, leaving behind large quantities of supplies, ammunition, and equipment. By sundown of the following day U. S. Marines were in possession of the Lunga airfield and had finished mopping up the forces at Gavutu and Tulagi, where fierce resistance was encountered. Caught off-guard initially, the enemy soon responded with air attacks on the invading forces. During the first 2 days of action, American carrier-based aircraft and antiaircraft batteries shot down 47 enemy planes. On the night of 8 August enemy surface forces moving in to disrupt unloading operations were intercepted by cruisers and destroyers; the ensuing battle off Savo Island resulted in the loss of four U. S. cruisers. By the following day most of the vessels in the invasion force had withdrawn, leaving the Marines to hold their gains.

The ferocity of belated enemy opposition had already indicated something of what was in store for the American forces. A period of relative quiet following the Savo Island action was broken on 24 August by the Battle of the Eastern Solomons, when combined American forces halted an enemy attempt to retake Guadalcanal. B-17's of the 11th Group, planes of the carrier Saratoga, Marine aircraft based on Guadalcanal, and surface vessels were credited with sinking a Japanese carrier, 4 warships, and 2 submarines, destroying 90 enemy aircraft, and damaging additional planes and vessels.

Throughout the month of August, the 11th Group carried out daily search missions over the lower Solomons, sometimes encountering enemy flying boats and fighters and usually emerging successfully from such encounters. By 20 August only 1 B-17 had been lost in combat and 2 had disappeared at sea, but 8 operational losses had been suffered. Lack of proper operating facilities, a scarcity of spare parts, tools, and equipment, and overworked personnel--along with the natural enervation of the South Pacific--all had their effect on the 11th Group. The location of squadrons in New Caledonia, the Fijis, and the New Hebrides and unreliable radio communications between the widely separated bases made operational control extremely difficult. At Espiritu Santo, the most forward base, Colonel Saunders maintained a command post, but operational facilities consisted largely of a narrow airstrip hacked out of a coconut grove and adjoining jungle. For early morning missions, crews were forced to mark the runway with jeep headlights and bottles of oil containing paper wicks. Officers and men slept under trees, wings, or inside the B-17's. Unloading facilities on the island were almost non-existent.

The 67th Fighter Squadron

On Guadalcanal the situation was no better. No heavy equipment had been landed on 7 August, and there was no harbor at Guadalcanal proper. By utilizing all the equipment left by the fleeing Japanese, however, the Marines quickly put the Lunga airfield into condition, renaming it Henderson Field in honor of the commander of Marine dive bombers at Midway. On the afternoon of 20 August 2 squadrons of Marine fighter planes arrived at Henderson, after being brought within 200 miles of Guadalcanal by aircraft carrier. Two days later 5 P-400's of the 67th Fighter Squadron, led by Capt. Dale D. Brannon, completed a series of long hops from New Caledonia via Efate and Espiritu to Henderson Field. Following the later arrival of part of the ground echelon and 9 more P-400's, the 67th Squadron went into action with Marine aircraft.

For the next few months the fate of Henderson Field hung in the balance. Enemy troops were close enough to maintain a constant threat, while snipers sometimes slipped through the perimeter defense and penetrated the field itself. The "Tokyo Express"--fast vessels loaded with men and supplies--almost nightly brought reinforcements to the Japanese troops on Guadalcanal and then shelled Henderson Field before withdrawing to the upper Solomons. Air attacks on the field occurred nearly every day. Against these determined enemy attempts, the Army

The Solomon Islands

and Marine airmen on Guadalcanal threw all their weight—slight though it was in comparison. It was soon discovered, here as earlier in the Southwest Pacific, that the P-400 was no match for enemy planes flying at high altitudes. After the first 4 days' operation at full strength only three of the original 14 P-400's remained in commission. General Vandegrift immediately revised the use of the plane, and before another month had passed the P-400 was proving to be invaluable when employed in close coordination with the Marine troops. Meanwhile, P-39K's in rear areas were being stripped of some of their equipment to give this later model fighter a service ceiling of 27,000 feet.

Daily operations took their toll of both fighters and bombers. Replacements were not available as fast as they were needed, and airmen in the South Pacific began to suspect strongly that they were in a forgotten theater of war. But officials in Washington were greatly concerned over the Solomons operations. While preparations for the invasion of North Africa enjoyed first priority, efforts were made to provide some relief for forces already face to face with the enemy; and in September General H. H. Arnold, Commanding General of the AAF, made a hurried visit to the Pacific theater in order to acquire first-hand information on the needs of the air forces. General Harmon was given authority to divert temporarily any bombers and crews en route to Australia, provided they could be used more effectively in the South Pacific Area. Furthermore, any aircraft and crews considered necessary for the Solomons operations could be requested from the Seventh Air Force by Adm. Chester W. Nimitz, Commander in Chief of the

Pacific Ocean Area. By mid-September, 15 P-38's had been diverted from the Southwest Pacific, and the 72d Squadron of the 5th Bombardment Group (H) had been ordered south from the Seventh Air Force, to be followed 1 month later by 2 additional squadrons of the same group. A small increase in fighter strength was authorized, and on 3 October the 347th Fighter Group was activated, being composed of the new 339th Squadron and the 67th, 68th, and 70th Fighter Squadrons already in the South Pacific.

The Crisis

While incoming air units were being hurriedly trained for operations in the forward area, defending forces on Guadalcanal were fighting for their very existence. During October—the crucial month in the Solomons Campaign—land, sea, and air fighting reached a peak of intensity, and Henderson Field was all but lost to the enemy. By the end of September the Japanese had put ashore almost an entire new division, and heavier concentrations of enemy shipping further indicated an impending battle for Guadalcanal. In early October an American naval task force moved north from Espiritu Santo in an effort to halt the Tokyo Express. The resulting engagement on 11 October, known as the Battle of Cape Esperance, dealt the enemy surface forces their heaviest losses since the Midway action; but the Express was not stopped. Two days later Japanese warships moved in and shelled Henderson Field so thoroughly that almost every plane on Guadalcanal was either destroyed or damaged. Near Kokumbona, 10 miles west, approximately 16,000 enemy troops poured ashore, opposed from the air by only 10 American planes.

The Marines, on the other hand, were shortly reinforced with the 164th Regimental Combat Team of the Army's Americal Division, stationed at New Caledonia. Also at Henderson Field was the 6th Navy Construction Battalion which was adept at keeping the runway in operable condition. Lack of gasoline kept most of the undamaged aircraft on the ground, but on 15 October two Marine transport squadrons and the 13th Troop Carrier Squadron of the AAF began to ferry in fuel. Patched-up planes then bombed and strafed enemy troops streaming ashore between Kokumbone and Doma Reef. In between missions the airmen spent their time in fox-holes, which at best offered only dubious shelter from Japanese bombs and shells. Many officers and men cracked under the strain. It was clear that the issue of Henderson Field would be decided soon.

Vice Adm. William F. Halsey, Jr., who became commander of the South Pacific Area on 20 October, prepared to cut off the enemy thrust by sea. But the decision was reached on the ridges of Guadalcanal. The major land assault against American lines came on 23 to 26 October. Only by vigorous counterattacks were the Japanese pushed back on the 26th. At the same time, a powerful naval force moving down from the mandated islands was shadowed by B-17's and PBY's flying out from Espiritu. American naval forces and all available aircraft then engaged the enemy in the Battle of Santa Cruz Islands, resulting in serious damage to surface units of both forces and--more important--resulting in withdrawal of the crippled enemy. Further offensive attempts were made by the enemy in mid-November, but two intense naval engagements again sent the Japanese survivors retreating northward.

Throughout the bitter fighting of previous weeks, the 67th Fighter Squadron joined with Marine aircraft to hit at enemy troops, landing barges, and supplies on Guadalcanal, while B-17's worked out of Espiritu on search and bombing missions whenever enemy targets came within range. With the mid-November turning point in the Solomons Campaign, B-17's could greatly increase their effectiveness by staging from Henderson Field. Distant enemy targets in the northernmost Solomons now began to feel the blows of the heavy bombers. A Navy construction battalion had begun work on another bomber strip at Koli, approximately 12 miles from Henderson Field. On 12 November the 339th Fighter Squadron, bringing its new P-38's from rear bases, had landed on a fighter strip just east of Henderson, and on the following day eight P-38's belonging to Southwest Pacific forces flew in non-stop from Milne Bay, to add much-needed fighter strength to the Solomons forces. All air units now began to strike at the Slender Express which continued to run but which was never again able to bring in sufficient enemy forces for a sustained threat against Henderson Field.

American forces on Guadalcanal could now turn their attention to an offensive. The battle-weary Marines were replaced by two Army divisions, the Americal and the 25th, and by the fresh 6th Marine Regiment. Maj. Gen. Alexander M. Patch succeeded General Vandegrift as commander of the Guadalcanal-Tulagi area. The AAF was to continue operating in accordance with the pattern set earlier in the campaign, but with better operating facilities and increased effectiveness.

Before the end of December, authority was given for organization of the AAF units into a new air force, to be headed by Brig. Gen. Nathan F. Twining. Appropriately enough, formal activation of the Thirteenth Air Force was delayed until 1300 hours, 13 January 1943. More important than any organizational change was the fact that a sound apprenticeship had been served in Army-Navy relations, and the combined efforts of American forces had succeeded in placing the enemy definitely on the defensive in the South Pacific.

THE FIFTH AIR FORCE IN NEW GUINEA

American landings in the Solomons had been prompted by a belief in offense as the best defense. The same tenet was held by Allied commanders in the Southwest Pacific, though forces were available for nothing more than a limited offensive. During the lull which followed the Coral Sea action, plans were under consideration for recapture of Rabaul and for seizure of Buna, a former administrative center on the northern coast of Papua. The Allied Air Forces were scheduled to play an important part in both actions. Siezure of the Buna area, which offered the most suitable location for an air base, was regarded as a prerequisite to control of the northern New Guinea coast--a move which in turn was prerequisite to more ambitious undertakings in the Bismarck Archipalago.

Early in July 1942, a reconnaissance party began a precarious trek over the lofty Owen Stanley mountains, expecting to reach Buna and to survey a site for an air base by the end of the month. But on 21 July, Japanese forces landed just north of Buna, and initiated the Papuan Campaign, which dragged on for 6 months over some of the wildest terrain in the Southwest Pacific. Operations by the Allied Air Forces, though limited by small resources, nevertheless proved to be one of the decisive factors in successful termination of the campaign by the end of January 1943. The operations were by no means consistently successful; but through tactical experiments and materiel modifications, the Allied Air Forces adapted their weapons to the immediate situation, with the result that a workable pattern was outlined for further operations in the Southwest Pacific. The Papuan action was, in a sense, a proving ground for both tried and untried tactics, and in the words of Gen. Douglas C. MacArthur, "The outstanding military lesson of this campaign was the continuous, calculated application of air power, inherent in the potentialities of every component of the air forces, employed in the most intimate tactical and logistical union with ground troops."

At the time of the Japanese landing, Allied forces under General MacArthur were organized in substantially the same commands as had been established on 18 April 1942, with air and ground troops making up the bulk of the forces. Gen. Sir Thomas Blamey, veteran Australian leader, headed the Allied Land Forces, which included, in addition to the Australian militia, almost two divisions recently returned from the Middle East, and the American 32d and 41st Divisions. The command originally set up as "U. S. Army Forces in Australia" was reorganized on 20 July as U. S. Services of Supply in the Southwest Pacific, under Brig. Gen. Richard J. Marshall. On the same date Allied Headquarters in the Southwest Pacific was moved from Melbourne to Brisbane, in keeping with the expected development of more extensive operations north of the continent.

Units of the Allied Air Forces, commanded by Lt. Gen. George H. Brett, were likewise moving northward in Australia, though as yet not all of the allotted strength had arrived from the United States. The burden of heavy bombardment was still carried by the 19th Group, while the 43d Group awaited the arrival of its air echelon. Of the two medium bombardment groups only one, the 22d, was engaging in combat; the 38th Group (minus the 69th and 70th Squadrons, which were in the South Pacific) did not begin extensive operations in Australia until mid-September. The 3d Bombardment Group (L) was flying A-24's, A-20's, and B-25's. The 49th Fighter Group was still defending the Darwin area with P-40's, while the 8th Group, equipped with P-39's, and the 35th Group, equipped with P-400's, were rotating their squadrons between Port Moresby and air bases in northeastern Australia. Also in operation were the 21st and 22d Troop Carrier Squadrons, incompletely equipped, and Flight "A" of the 8th Photographic Squadron.

The active RAAF component of the Allied Air Forces was relatively small, though an ambitious expansion program was under way. Of the 30 RAAF squadrons only 3 were equipped with P-40's, the remainder being provided largely with training planes and outmoded patrol and transport aircraft. For replacement of outmoded types and implementation of the expansion program, the Australians were looking primarily to the United States. The third component of the Allied Air Forces consisted of one squadron of B-25's manned by Netherlands East Indies flyers, though additional NEI units were being trained in the United States for eventual participation in the Southwest Pacific action.

Such was the strength of the command to which Maj. Gen. George C. Kenney acceded on 4 August 1942. General Kenney found somewhat the same problems facing him as had faced General Brett in the spring.

Shortages of tools, aircraft parts, and trained mechanics, heavy combat demands, and weather and distance factors made it difficult for the 6 air base and 2 air depot groups to keep even 50 per cent of available aircraft in commission. Combat fatigue, casualties, and lack of immediate replacements were still chief personnel problems, while a rigid training program required the services of a number of experienced airmen. In addition, the Allied Air Forces were now confronted with a new tactical situation--a determined enemy moving overland to Port Moresby, the one remaining Allied base in New Guinea.

The Japanese had ample reason for desiring to add Port Moresby to their growing list of conquests. For the same reason, Allied forces in the Southwest Pacific could not afford to lose the base, for without it they could not bomb distant enemy strongholds in the Bismarck Archipelago. During the summer of 1942 Port Moresby was the scene of bustling activity, as construction forces improved existing airfields and built new ones. The town itself was situated on a narrow coastal plain only a few miles from the jungle. For protection of Port Moresby the Allied commanders had to rely chiefly on a few fighter squadrons and the physical features of Papua. Both terrain and weather were so formidable as to make air operations difficult and ground operations almost impossible. The forbidding Owen Stanley Range, with many of its snow-capped peaks rising almost 3 miles into the air, formed a veritable mountain wall between the northern and southern coasts of Papua. Overland crossings could be made only by foot over crude native tracks which transversed treacherous mountain streams and rivers, thick jungle undergrowth, and narrow mountain passes. One of the tracks from Port Moresby led through "the Gap," a pass some 5,000 to 8,000 feet above sea level, and emerged at the villages of Isurava and Deniki just short of Kokoda. From this point, halfway between Port Moresby and Buna, the track continued for 63 miles over rolling but relatively easy terrain. Torrential rainfalls, however, kept tracks impassable much of the time.

Air transportation provided the swiftest means of crossing the mountains. Along the level coastal belt, temporary landing strips could easily be made by cutting patches of the tall tropical grasses; before the outbreak of war such strips were in use at Kokoda, Buna, and other of the more important government stations. But flights over the Owen Stanleys were frequently limited by adverse weather conditions, including dangerous thunderheads which sometimes rose to 40,000 feet above sea level. Allied flyers who encountered such conditions, if unable to surmount or circumvent the clouds, were forced to return to Port Moresby. Those who succeeded in flying through were usually thrown about inside the plane, and if fortunate, they returned with no more serious injuries than broken arms or legs. Added to weather hazards on bombing missions was the fatigue factor involved in long flights from bases on the Australian continent to Port Moresby, over the mountains, and thence to enemy targets. Such missions required from 36 to 48 hours away from the home base, with as much as 18 hours flying time over distances ranging up to 2,200 miles. The efficiency of both planes and flyers suffered; greater distances meant smaller bomb loads, and targets could not be hit with either the force or frequency demanded by the situation.

Such circumstances were impelling the Allies to seek air bases along the northern coast of Papua. The same conditions which hampered Allied operations also served somewhat to restrict enemy operations, and it was likewise logical for the Japanese to press for bases along the southern coast. Their sea-borne attempt in May had failed, but it was still possible for them to repeat the effort. As for an overland drive, the virtually impassable Owen Stanleys seemed to provide a barrier against any but the most desperate or fanatical enemy. Allied forces in the Southwest Pacific learned during the latter half of 1942 that they were faced with just such an enemy.

Buna-Kokoda, 21 July to 25 August

Two days before the Japanese landing at Buna, Allied aerial reconnaissance had disclosed a convoy near Rabaul. As the force moved toward the Buna area, Allied air units were marshaled at Port Moresby for opposition to the expected landing on the northern coast. Bombing efforts on the afternoon of 21 July were not too successful, as darkness closed in upon the planes soon after 1 B-17 and 5 B-26's located the targets. One direct hit was observed on a large transport, but the 4 destroyers and 1 cruiser were undeterred in their precautionary shelling of the area. During the night a landing was made at Gona, 12 miles north of Buna, and antiaircraft guns were quickly set up.

On the morning of 22 July, 3 heavy bomber, 5 medium bomber, and 5 fighter strikes were made on the convoy offshore, and on barges,

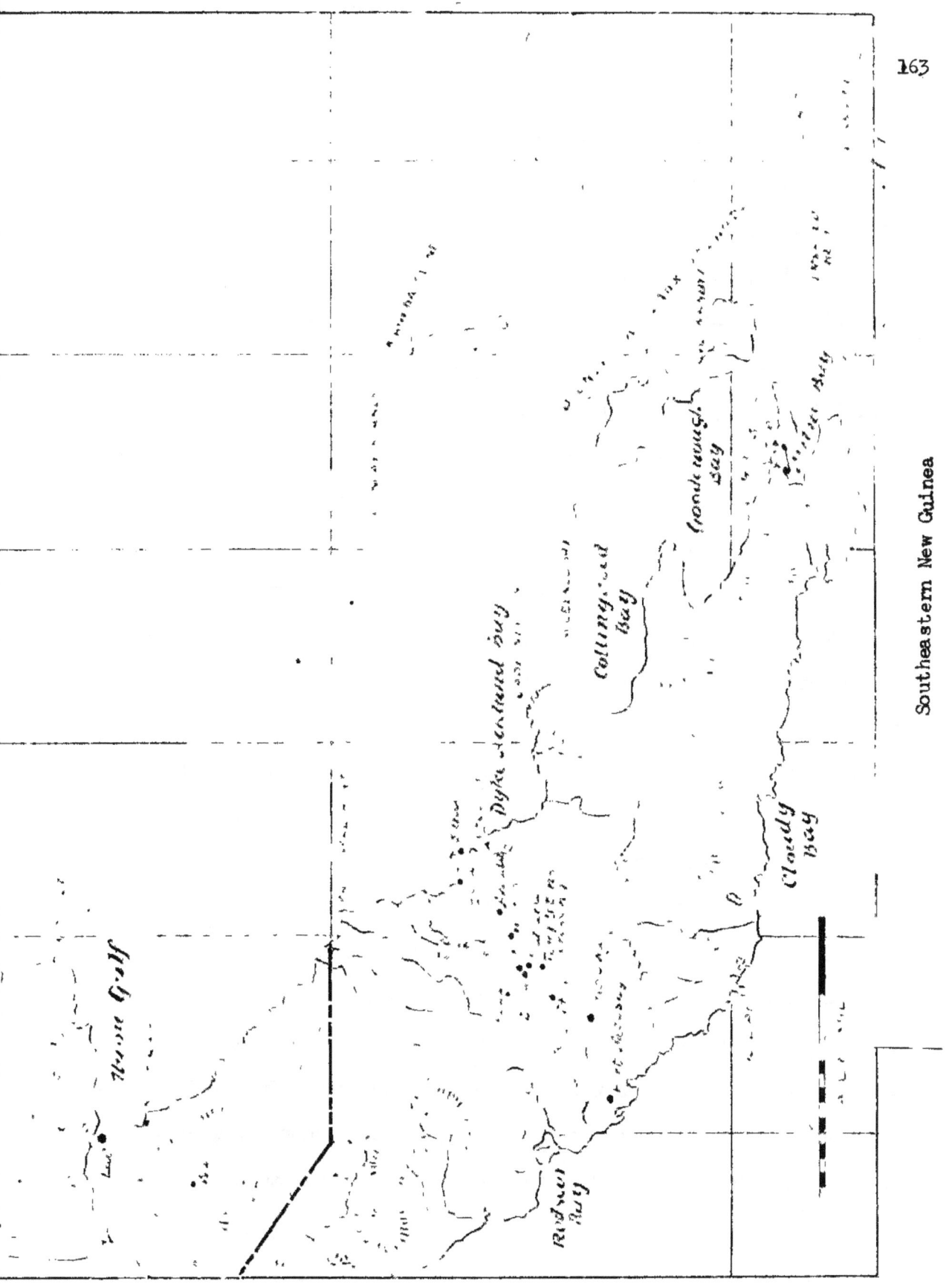

supplies, and personnel on the beaches. Heavy antiaircraft and machine gun fire kept the bombers high, though there was little air opposition. By the afternoon of the 22d, 1 large transport and 1 barge had been sunk, 1 destroyer damaged, and undetermined losses suffered from strafing; but the Japanese had succeeded in landing between 4,000 and 5,000 men. The enemy pushed rapidly inland toward Kokoda, where sole opposition was provided by an Australian militia unit which had worked its way up from Port Moresby.

While the Australians were being gradually forced back from Kokoda to Deniki and Isurava, gateway to the Gap, the Allied Air Forces carried out numerous and diversified tasks. Demands upon the forces were now far greater than they had been early in July when plans were made for aerial action in coordination with the Solomons offensive; but despite the new threat to Port Moresby, the Allied air units continued to strike at Rabaul and enemy bases in the upper Solomons. In addition, long-range reconnaissance planes kept a close watch on enemy shipping along the New Guinea coast. During the latter part of July and throughout August heavy, medium, and light bombers flew out of Port Moresby to oppose the landing of reinforcements in the Buna area, but the Japanese took advantage of darkness and adverse flying weather to render bombing attacks only partially successful. For bombing missions against Lae, Salamaua, and enemy positions nearer Port Moresby, Allied commanders depended chiefly upon the B-25's of the 3d Group and the B-26's of the 22d Group, although during August there were never more than 12 B-25's and 27 B-26's in commission.

On the continent of Australia and at Port Moresby, fighter units of the Allied Air Forces were of course still charged with defense of bases which were subject to enemy air attack. Both Darwin and Port Moresby were frequently bombed; and while the P-39's, P-40's, and P-400's were still unable to operate effectively at high altitudes, the fighters took their toll of enemy aircraft which came within range. If the American planes were less maneuverable than the Zero, they at least were more rugged and were able to outdive the Japanese plane. Fighter pilots, urged by General Kenney to make the most of these advantages, were gradually gaining confidence in their aircraft.

Other demands upon both fighters and bombers limited the amount of direct cooperation with ground forces during the Buna-Kokoda phase of the campaign, yet in this connection significant experiments were made which bore fruit during the latter phases of the Papuan action. One of the earliest successful fighter-bomber attacks occurred on 7 August when 32 old P-400's flew through the Gap on a mission against enemy supply dumps in the Kokoda area. The planes expended 25,000 rounds of ammunition in strafing the targets, while 16 of the fighters, carrying 500-pound bombs in improvised racks, dive-bombed under the cover of the remaining planes. Dive-bombing attacks by the slow and poorly-armed A-24 were not attempted after an experience on 29 July when only 1 out of 7 A-24's returned from a mission with P-39 escort. The other light bomber type in the Southwest Pacific, the A-20, was undergoing radical modifications which would greatly increase its efficiency.

Perhaps even more promising for the success of operations in New Guinea was the use of transport planes to bring in supplies. The Australians who were being forced back along the track from Kokoda were in need of a more rapid system of supply than that provided by the Papuan natives--though the value of their efforts could hardly be overestimated. The possibilities of air transport had already been demonstrated in the supplying of a small isolated force of Australians still fighting near Wau, inland from Lae and Salamaua. Extensive use of the method was now limited by the shortage of transport planes, the absence of suitable landing strips in the interior, and the lack of proper equipment; but supplies were flown in to the Kokoda strip until its loss, while L-5's brought supplies to another strip at Myola, approximately 15 miles south of Kokoda, until further enemy advances interrupted operations there on 17 August. A measure of success was attained in dropping supplies from transport planes, though not without initial failures. In order to put the supplies in the desired spot, pilots discovered that they had to fly at tree-top height, an extremely hazardous procedure in the mountainous region. Furthermore, in the absence of parachute equipment, which was not immediately available from the United States, it was necessary to use ordinary bags as containers; and until three thicknesses were used, the bags invariably split open on contact with the ground. Wrapping the supplies in Australian wool blankets and rope proved to be a still more successful method.

Milne Bay, 25 August to 10 September

The Allied Air Forces gained valuable experience in almost every phase of operations during the first month of the campaign, but the Japanese still had not been stopped. They were pursuing a vigorous and aggressive course of action in both the South and Southwest Pacific, building new airstrips and flying in more aerial reinforcements; and in mid-August there were indications of a major effort against Port Moresby, with possible parachute landings there or near Milne Bay, at the southeastern tip of New Guinea. Possession of this strategic area, guarding the sea-approaches from the Solomon Sea to New Guinea, was as vital to the Allies as to the Japanese. In the race for control of the area there was no duplication of the Buna experience, for General MacArthur's forces beat the enemy to Milne Bay and thereby achieved the first Allied victory of the Papuan Campaign--a victory which was clearly the result of careful planning and skillful execution.

By the end of the third week in August, when Japanese planes began their preliminary reconnaissance over Milne Bay, sizable American and Australian forces had been moved into the swampy area. There they had constructed airstrips; two RAAF P-40 squadrons and a few Hudsons had been placed at an airfield somewhat inland from the north shore; and the 8th Fighter Control Squadron had set up warning facilities at the field and on near-by Goodenough and Normanby islands.

The actual size of the Allied garrison apparently was unknown to the Japanese, for on 26 August they landed only about 2,000 men--a comparatively small force--along the northern shore of Milne Bay. The landing was made early in the morning under the cover of unseasonable weather, which limited the effectiveness of RAAF fighters attempting to dive-bomb the convoy. The Japanese, on the other hand, were undoubtedly deprived of much of their expected air cover, as P-400's from Port Moresby kept the Buna airstrip and its dispersed planes under fire on 25 and 26 August, destroying almost a score of Zeros which might otherwise have been used to cover the landing at Milne Bay.

Supported by shell fire from warships, the Japanese drove toward the Milne Bay airfield, making their greatest advances during the night and leaving small groups of snipers in the rear to hinder daytime counterattacks. RAAF P-40's concentrated on suspected positions of snipers, on landing barges, and on a few tanks—rapidly becoming bogged down in 4 to 6 feet of mud—while B-17's attacked vessels offshore. After reaching the airfield, the Japanese were rolled back by Australian infantry and American engineers whose infiltration and encircling movements were rapidly making the enemy position hopeless.

On 29 August the Japanese tacitly admitted the failure of their assault by evacuating large numbers of their forces in warships which still seemed to elude attacking aircraft. Only mopping-up activities remained for the Allies. The entire action was costly for both sides. From 700 to 1,000 Japanese were killed and 9 were captured, while Allied casualties numbered approximately 2,000, most of them resulting from malaria. The brevity of the Milne Bay action was by no means an indication of its importance, for the left prong of the pincers grasping for Port Moresby had been cut off and the Japanese had suffered their first notable defeat in New Guinea.

Kokoda-Iorabaiwa Ridge, 25 August to 2 November

Along the Kokoda track, however, the Japanese were still pushing toward their objective. By the middle of September they had driven the Australians through the Gap to Iorabaiwa Ridge, only 30 miles from Port Moresby. Enemy supply lines, now dangerously extended, became the object of repeated aerial attacks. Every available plane in the Allied Air Forces was thrown into the assault on communication lines in New Guinea, on vessels bringing supplies and reinforcements to the northern coast, and on key supply points in New Britain and the Solomons. The enemy took advantage of darkness and unseasonable weather to land reinforcements at Buna. From this point, native carriers and mules were used to transport supplies over almost 100 miles of jungle and mountain terrain to the front at Iorabaiwa. As soon as the 8th Photographic Squadron located corrals and new supply dumps, A-20's, modified for increased fire-power and range, proceeded to bomb and strafe the targets. Similar attacks, usually with fighter cover, were made against enemy ground forces, while aircraft with greater range crippled the enemy's air forces by destroying planes and damaging airfields at Buna, Lae, Salamaua, and Rabaul.

The desire of air commanders to hit targets in New Guinea with as much force as possible sometimes led to "unorthodox" use of certain types of planes. B-17's, for example, joined with shorter-range aircraft to bomb the Wairopi bridge spanning the Kumusi River, but heavy bombers had more success in the long-range attacks for which they were designed. On the other hand, the trial-and-error method led to the development of tactics and items of materiel which proved eminently successful in later phases of the campaign. Complications hindering the use of fragmentation bombs, for example, were overcome by equipping the bombs with parachutes, thus giving low-flying planes time to leave the target area before explosions occurred.

Whatever the contribution of Allied air operations during this crucial stage of the Papuan Campaign, the Japanese began to withdraw from Iorabaiwa Ridge, and on 2 November reinforced Australian troops pushed them out of Kokoda, placing the small but important airfield once again in Allied hands. The defensive stage of the campaign was clearly at an end. General MacArthur's forces were now ready to begin an offensive which was to be as successful in its outcome, though not as brief in duration, as the Milne Bay action.

Buna

While plans for the offensive were being perfected in the fall of 1942, the Allied Air Forces were undergoing a reorganization designed to clarify the responsibilities and increase the effectiveness of American and Australian components. Certain administrative difficulties which had existed since the formation of the Allied Air Forces were eliminated by the organization of American units into a typical air force, with bomber, fighter, and air base commands and all headquarters under American officers. Such a step could not have been taken earlier because of the shortage of experienced personnel. On 3 September the new unit was designated the Fifth Air Force, a designation formerly given to the Far East Air Force. General Kenney assumed command of the Fifth and also retained command of the Allied Air Forces. Under this arrangement he had administrative control of American air units in the Southwest Pacific and operational control of both American and Australian forces, while the RAAF was responsible for administration of its own units.

At Port Moresby, where at least seven airfields were in operation by November, an advanced echelon was established under Maj. Gen. Ennis C. Whitehead, deputy commander for General Kenney. Brig. Gen. Kenneth N. Walker, who had participated in numerous missions, became commander of the V Bomber Command, while the V Fighter Command was headed after 11 November by Col. Paul B. Wurtsmith, who had led the 49th Fighter Group in defense of the Darwin area.

In a division of operational duties, the RAAF was made responsible for defending the entire Australian continent with the exception of the Northeastern Area. This area, from which the planned offensive was to be launched, was entrusted to the Fifth Air Force. So flexible was the arrangement, however, that certain RAAF units frequently participated in missions with American squadrons, and Fifth Air Force planes often staged out of the Northwestern Area for operations against enemy positions in the Netherlands East Indies.

Oddly enough, it was the weakest element—numerically speaking— of the Fifth Air Force which was scheduled to figure most prominently in the coming offensive. The 21st and 22d Troop Carrier Squadrons, equipped with only some 40 planes, had moved most of the American 32d Division to Port Moresby in September. For still further moves and the supply of troops in Papua a much larger force of transports would be needed; by the end of October the two squadrons had only 62 planes. At AAF headquarters in Washington, concern over the situation led to allocation of the 6th and 33d Troop Carrier Squadrons to the Fifth Air Force. On 1 November the 374th Troop Carrier Group was activated, to be composed of the two squadrons already in the Southwest Pacific and the two which were expected to arrive shortly.

The first large-scale troop-ferrying movement in the theater, however, had to be carried out by the transports on hand; there was no time to wait for the expected arrivals. On 6 October the 21st and 22d Squadrons began extensive operations for the new phase of the campaign: an Australian infantry battalion was flown to an airstrip on the northwestern shore of Collingwood Bay, within 65 miles of Buna. The Australians, soon joined by a party of American engineers, hacked out a series of airstrips along the coast southeast of Buna. Between 14 October and 10 November the transport planes carried to the northern coast of Papua a company of Australian troops and two regiments of the 32d Division.

Announced almost simultaneously with the North African invasion, the troop-ferrying feat in the Southwest Pacific naturally received little notice at the time. Yet in view of the possibilities inherent in aerial transportation of combat troops as demonstrated by the accomplishment, in view of subsequent uses on an even larger scale in other theaters, and in view of its immediate effect on the situation in New Guinea, its importance could hardly be exaggerated.

Food, ammunition, and other supplies were still being dropped to ground troops along the track, while vast quantities of supplies, including heavy artillery, were flown to the forces advancing toward Buna from the southeast. All available planes, including B-25's, were being used, and on return trips many of the aircraft evacuated casualties to Port Moresby. During the final 2 months of the campaign air evacuation averaged over 100 men daily, reaching a peak of 280 on 8 December. Heavy rains, rough landing strips, and overworked planes and personnel made the transport operations hazardous; the additional danger of enemy attacks was usually eliminated by fighter cover.

Bombers of the Fifth Air Force were still hitting at enemy convoys and distant bases, though under difficult circumstances. Only by means of many extra hours' work could ground crews of the 19th and 43d Groups keep a daily average of 40 heavy bombers in commission. What the air force lacked in strength, its commanders attempted to compensate for by improved techniques. Under the direction of Maj. William G. Benn, the bomber command practiced low-level attacks on shipping. Eight .50-cal. machine guns were added to the nose of the B-25, and the resulting combination of tremendous fire power and "skip-bombing" began to pay dividends in the latter days of the Papuan Campaign. In fact, skip-bombing proved so far superior to aerial torpedo attacks that the training program for the latter was dropped in the Southwest Pacific.

To the problem of perfecting new techniques in the midst of the campaign was added the problem of training an entirely new heavy bombardment group and of maintaining a new type of plane in the theater. In line with a headquarters decision to replace all B-17's in the Pacific with the longer-range B-24's, the 90th Bombardment Group was sent to Australia during October and November, equipped with Liberators. The move involved no increase in strength for the Fifth Air Force, as the war-weary 19th Group was returned to the United States for a well-earned rest. Until the 90th Group completed its training and began extensive combat operations late in December, the 43d Group with its B-17's carried out heavy bombardment missions.

In coordination with ground forces, light and medium bombers and fighter planes continued to attack retreating enemy troops. Success of the attacks could not easily be determined, for flyers often found themselves bombing clumps of heavy foliage--just as the ground troops were constantly shooting at an enemy well-concealed in trees or behind jungle undergrowth. While Allied pressure along the Kokoda track, dive-bombing and strafing of enemy troops and supply lines, and attacks on convoys and distant bases all contributed to the turn in the battle, it was undoubtedly the enveloping movement of American and Australian troops around the Buna area which caused the Japanese to retrace their steps so quickly. In order to prevent the isolation of their troops along the track, the Japanese rapidly fell back and took up well-defended positions at three coastal villages--Buna, Gona, and Sanananda. Reorganized American ground forces, under the command of Lt. Gen. Robert L. Eichelberger, and fresh Australian forces early in December began what were essentially siege operations. Gona was overrun on 9 December, and Allied forces then concentrated on isolating the two remaining garrisons.

By the end of December it was obvious that the Papuan Campaign was nearing its close; the fall of Buna was only 3 days away, and the fate of enemy troops at Sanananda would be sealed after 3 more weeks. The fighting on the ground and in the air had not been easy. Casualties had been extremely heavy, with tropical diseases accounting for almost 8 times the casualties caused from wounds. Prompt evacuation by air was perhaps the only encouraging aspect of the situation.

As for the Fifth Air Force, the outlook at the end of 1942 was better than at any time since the beginning of hostilities in the Southwest Pacific. True, there had been no substantial increase in aerial strength, nor had there been any great advance in terms of miles. But air bases now existed along the northeastern coast of New Guinea, shortening the distance to enemy targets and allowing fighter cover for bombing operations. High-flying P-38's were being supplied in increasing numbers; overwhelming success in their first reported combat in the Southwest Pacific on 27 December proved that the Lightnings were the answer to the Japanese Zero. Furthermore, AAF units in the South Pacific had joined in attacks on Rabaul on 25 December, relieving the Fifth Air Force of part of its bombing responsibilities but making more certain the eventual neutralization of this enemy stronghold.

Even more significant, the Fifth had become a versatile air force, in response to the varied demands of the theater. There was no single well-defined mission such as that guiding the Eighth Air Force; peculiarities of the Southwest Pacific theater called for employment of every capability of air power. In learning to adapt their weapons and tactics to the immediate demands, air commanders in the Southwest Pacific had discovered a successful formula for combatting the enemy.

-III

THE ELEVENTH AIR FORCE IN THE ALEUTIANS

In the North Pacific, Japanese forces, following their abortive attack on Dutch Harbor in June, retired to the western islands of Kiska and Attu, and aerial warfare in the Aleutians settled down to a fairly routine course. Attempting to prevent the consolidation and expansion of enemy positions, the Eleventh Air Force during the remainder of the summer bombed and strafed Japanese installations whenever weather permitted. Enemy efforts apparently were concentrated on preparation of defenses against expected air attacks from the Umnak base, as enemy positions were beginning to bristle with heavy and medium flak batteries. The Eleventh Air Force, on the other hand, concentrated on offensive efforts, increasing the strength of air units and reorganizing forces to meet the tactical situation.

Augmentation of the air force, which had begun immediately prior to the Dutch Harbor attack, was continued with the addition of as many squadrons as could be spared from the United States. Before 1 July the 406th Bombardment Squadron with its B-25's had arrived at Elmendorf Field, and the 54th Fighter Group (and the 56th and 57th Fighter Squadrons) had been attached to the XI Fighter Command. The provisional XI Bomber Command, headed by Col. William O. Eareckson, was activated on 1 July, being made up of the 28th Composite Group and its assigned squadrons. One week later the 404th Bombardment

Squadron arrived in Alaska; its B-24's, originally destined for the North African theater, were painted with a pink camouflage--ideal for desert warfare but clearly unsuited for the Alaskan theater. The squadron was immediately dubbed "The Pink Elephants" and sent to Nome to patrol the Bering Sea north of the Seward Peninsula.

Inasmuch as the arrival of tactical units and their dispersal to widely separated bases created new service troop demands, the War Department allocated one additional service group and six air base squadrons to supplement the 23d Service Group and 24th Air Base Squadron already in Alaska. Formation of the XI Air Force Service Command, under Brig. Gen. Robert V. Ignico, was a logical step toward more effective operation of depots, bases, and stations.

Organizational details, problems of air strength, and even the Japanese themselves gave the Eleventh Air Force considerably less trouble than did the Alaskan weather. Forecasts were of little use to the flyers, since the weather conditions could change more rapidly than planes could fly. After the Dutch Harbor attack it became standard practice for one of the heavy bombers, acting as a weather plane, to take off from Umnak early each morning and fly more than 600 miles to reconnoiter the Kiska area. If conditions were favorable, the information was radioed to Umnak and immediately other bombers took off to attack. More often than not, missions had to be cancelled on account of the weather. In July, for example, there were only 15 days when the weather plane could advise formations of heavy bombers to proceed with the attack. Even then, on seven occasions the planes were forced to return to Umnak because of the weather. Flyers who succeeded in getting through to the target were generally forced by the low-ceiling and poor visibility to bomb from a low altitude or to make their bomb runs by dead-reckoning, taking their bearings from an old volcanic crater which was virtually the only landmark in the outer islands.

To Brig. Gen. William O. Butler, commander of the Eleventh Air Force, and to other airmen in the theater it was obvious that such sporadic operations could never drive the enemy out of the Aleutians. On missions to Kiska the B-17's and B-24's could carry little more than half a load of bombs, (3,500-pounds), for the 1,200-mile round trip required bomb bay tanks. The great distance also meant that bombers could have no fighter protection. Fighters were used only for patrols around Umnak and the seaplane base at Nazan Bay, Atka Island, some 300 miles from Umnak. Only when a few Japanese float-planes would venture to this point did the fighters have any opportunity to make contact with the enemy, who still had no facilities on Kiska for operating land-based planes. Both the Americans and the Japanese were faced with the problem of securing bases nearer to the enemy so that fighter protection could be provided on bombing missions and bombers could deliver more forceful attacks. Before the end of summer the Japanese were reported reconnoitering Adak and Amchitka and other potential bases between Kiska and Umnak. Fortunately, American forces moved more swiftly.

Adak

At midnight on 29 August a small party of intelligence scouts slipped up to the island of Adak by means of rubber boats launched from submarines. Between periods of hiding from enemy reconnaissance planes the group surveyed the mountainous island and discovered several tidal flats suitable for airfields. Other assets were found: dunes, which would afford natural protection for aircraft, and a good inner harbor with deep water. The surveying party signaled to watchful PBY's which in turn carried word back to the task force waiting at Cold Bay. At dawn on the 31st the convoy moved in upon Adak, and under the cover of Eleventh Air Force planes, construction engineers set to work on an airfield which was completed in record-breaking time. On 10 September the first plane, an old B-18A, landed on the steel-mat runway. By the evening of the 13th the Adak hardstands were covered by 15 B-24's, 1 B-17, 15 P-38's, and 16 P-39's. The last raid on Kiska from Umnak was made on the 13th, and on the following day the first major attack was launched from Adak. Twelve B-24's, whose crews had been practicing low-level bombing, were led by Colonel Eareckson in a heavy assault on Kiska harbor, while 14 P-38's and 14 P-39's strafed shore installations, batteries, and the camp area.

The attack of 14 September inaugurated a new phase of the Aleutian campaign. The air war now increased in tempo and intensity, for the Adak base cut down the striking distance between the opponents by about one half. Attacks were made by both medium and heavy bombers of the Eleventh Air Force, frequently with fighter escort. Japanese float-planes made a few retaliatory raids on Adak, but the enemy was never allowed to take the offensive. During the fall months enemy plans seemed somewhat uncertain, as troops were evacuated from Attu to Kiska in September and then moved back to Attu in November. Eleventh Air Force targets during this period included shipping between the two islands, antiaircraft batteries, the Kiska submarine base, hangars, and camp installations. In combat with enemy planes the American fighters destroyed an average of half the fighter opposition encountered, while bombers constantly hammered at newly-assembled planes in Holtz Bay, Attu, thereby whittling Japanese air strength in the Aleutians down to an ineffectual force.

The race for island bases was not over with American occupation of Adak. The Eleventh Air Force needed other bases near Kiska, and the enemy undoubtedly wanted sites more suitable for land-based aircraft. Only a shortage of construction personnel and equipment hindered American action. The project to build an airfield on Atka, just east of Adak, had to be delayed until after work was well under way at Adak. On 7 October excavation was begun at the new site and by the middle of November a steel-mat runway had been laid, giving the Eleventh Air Force two bases within fairly close range of the enemy.

The Japanese were now forced to take more aggressive action if they were to maintain their position off the North American continent. Late in November an enemy convoy was reported on its way to occupy the Semichis, which offered the best site for a landing field within effective distance of American forces; but when spotted by Navy patrol planes west of Attu the convoy reversed its course--perhaps because of over-cautious commanders or because the task force possessed less striking power than the situation required.

Amchitka

In December the Japanese were observed to be preparing for another aggressive move, apparently aimed this time at the island of Amchitka, 70 miles southeast of Kiska. Again, American forces moved more swiftly than enemy troops. On 18 December a small reconnaissance party set out from Adak to survey the island which lay almost under the very nose of the enemy. Within less than a month the first construction and ground troops were landed on Amchitka and work was begun on an airfield. From this point on, there was little doubt that the Japanese garrisons at Kiska and Attu were doomed.

In 6 months the Eleventh Air Force had moved almost 600 miles nearer to the enemy. Air operations still conformed to the simple pattern of hitting Japanese shipping and installations with every available weapon. Figures of bomb tonnage were not impressive when compared with those of much larger air forces in the European theater. During the peak month of October, for example, the Eleventh Air Force dropped only 200 tons of bombs. But constant pounding and strafing was proving to be a successful formula for air operations in the Alaskan theater.

In order to keep a maximum number of planes in the air, ground crews had worked in the severest kind of weather. Maintenance and repair work was necessarily performed out of doors, frequently with blinding rain and snow blowing in horizontal sheets. Engines were changed and battle damage repaired throughout many nights, with only flashlights and truck headlights for illumination. Certain spare parts could be obtained only by salvaging wrecked planes. Living conditions at advanced bases were primitive. Tents and small structures often collapsed under gale winds, while planes had to be tied down with oil drums. Dispersal areas were generally mud morasses, and roads were nothing more than tracks through the spongy muskeg.

If members of the Eleventh Air Force were not able to do anything about the Alaskan weather, they at least had proved that effective operations by land-based planes were possible in the theater. By the end of the year the air force was in a favorable position to carry out its mission. Fighter strength had been further increased by activation of the 344th Squadron of the 343d Fighter Group. Heavier air transport demands were being met by the newly-activated 54th Troop Carrier Squadron. Bombardment squadrons had gone far toward perfecting the technique of low-level bombing. The service command, which was composed of approximately half the personnel in the air force, had stationed air base squadrons at all important bases. Issues previously uncertain were clarified and service personnel were relieved of certain responsibilities in rear areas. Units of the Air Transport Command, for example, were moved in to staff bases along the new ATC route to Alaska. Certain service units at Ladd Field, the AAF cold weather station, were relieved of their assignment and moved to Elmendorf, where they could be of more assistance to the Eleventh Air Force.

Every unit of the Eleventh was now geared to the westward movement of American forces. The issue of mastery in the North Pacific was not yet settled, but it was no longer in doubt. The campaign had already proved the strategic importance of Alaska and the Aleutians--in previous years a debated subject--and it had demonstrated, as well, the value of land-based air power in that region.

THE TENTH AIR FORCE IN INDIA AND CHINA

Of all the air forces opposing the Japanese, perhaps none was faced with a more difficult situation than was the Tenth Air Force in the summer of 1942. The Americans were committed to a policy of maintaining air operations in China and supplying the Chinese with increasing quantities of war goods, yet Japanese conquest of Burma had closed all entrances to China except by way of the 18,000-foot Himalayas. Furthermore, the enemy was momentarily expected to push into India and, as soon as the heavy rains ceased in the fall, to interfere seriously with air communications "over the Hump." An emergency shifting of key officers, heavy bombers, and transport planes to the Middle East impaired the Tenth, and the few units arriving from the United States could not immediately compensate for the loss. Organizational equipment, spare parts, and replacements were still slow in arriving; the airfield construction program, depending to a large extent upon native hand labor, was far behind schedule; and in August political agitation in India resulted in riots, strikes, and demonstrations which continued over a period of many weeks, disrupting transportation and communications in large areas.

In spite of the unfavorable circumstances, air commanders in the China-Burma-India theater guided the Tenth Air Force through a series of significant developments, and before the end of 1942 the Japanese were made acutely aware of the fact that American air power could deliver blows on the Asiatic mainland comparable to those which were falling on Kiska, the Northern Solomons, and Northeast New Guinea.

When a German advance into Egypt in June precipitated a crisis for the defending British forces, General Brereton was ordered to take available bombers of the Tenth Air Force to the Middle East. Having been authorized to move all personnel, planes and equipment essential for operations, the commander of the Tenth Air Force left India on 26 June with General Adler and other key officers, while arrangements were made for the most experienced ferry pilots to transport supplies to the Middle East. General Brereton was soon followed by the 9th Bombardment Squadron, which had the only experienced heavy bombardment crews and ground personnel in India. The Tenth, seriously crippled by the sudden diversion, was left under the command of Brig. Gen. Earl L. Naiden.

The immediate task was to establish the projected China Air Task Force, to be composed of the 23d Fighter Group under the command of Col. Robert L. Scott and a small force of medium bombers under Col. Caleb V. Haynes. Command of the task force was given to Brig. Gen. Claire L. Chennault, whose American Volunteer Group of fighter pilots in less than 7 months had established the remarkable record of 298 enemy planes destroyed, with only 12 American pilots lost from enemy action. In accordance with a plan already agreed upon by Generalissimo Chiang Kai-shek, General Chennault, and other officials, the AVG was disbanded and its members were given an opportunity to be inducted into the AAF and to remain in China as part of the 23d Group. Most of the pilots were weary from months of active combat and some desired to return home for a brief rest; others who were former members of the Navy and Marine Corps naturally preferred to rejoin these branches of the service; still others chose to take positions with commercial air concerns. As a result, only 5 pilots and a small number of ground men of the AVG were inducted into the AAF on 4 July, but approximately 20 additional pilots remained on duty for 2 weeks until replacements could arrive.

Although the China Air Task Force made maximum use of the labor, materials, and supplies already available in China, its existence depended upon the development of an extensive air cargo service over the Himalayas. For some time the shortage of aircraft forced the 1st Ferry Group to operate on a "shoestring." During the summer months the volume of freight flown from India to China fell considerably below the volume carried in April and May, the highest estimate of deliveries during the monsoon period being 800 tons per month.

Brig. Gen. Clayton L. Bissell, who on 18 August succeeded General Naiden as commander of the Tenth Air Force, immediately turned his attention to the problems of developing a well-balanced air force, of supplying the forces in China, and of providing adequate defense for the Dinjan-Kunming ferry route, which was reputed to involve more hazards than any other regularly used route of comparable distance. In June it had been decided that American air combat forces in Asia should be composed of 1 heavy bombardment and

1 medium bombardment group and 2 fighter groups, but the Tenth Air Force was not scheduled to reach its authorized strength until October.

In the meantime, General Bissell sought means of improving the forces already in the theater and made preparations for the use of projected units. Chief among his plans was organization of all combat units in India into a task force similar to the one in China. In addition to the two task forces, the Tenth Air Force would then be composed of the Karachi American Air Base under Brig. Gen. Francis M. Brady, the X Air Force Service Command under Col. Robert C. Oliver, and the India-China Ferry Command under Col. Robert Tate. Until the India Air Task Force was activated early in October, however, the bulk of American air combat in the theater was provided by the task force in China.

China Air Task Force

During its first months of operation the China Air Task Force was composed of the 23d Fighter Group, the 16th Squadron of the 51st Fighter Group (on detached service), one flight of the 9th Photo Reconnaissance Squadron, and several flights of the 11th Squadron (M) of the 7th Bombardment Group. Operational aircraft numbered approximately 7 B-25's and 30 P-40's. With this small force, General Chennault faced the problem of conducting effective fighter and bomber operations along a 5,000-mile front extending from Chungking and Chengtu to the Indo-China Red River in the south, the Tibetan plateau and the Salween River in the west, and the China Sea in the east. Operations were conducted from a number of Chinese airfields, including Hengyang, Kweilin, and Nanning, in order to bring most of the important enemy targets in southern China within range of the B-25 and P-40. The aircraft also operated from Yunnanyi, in western China, and Dinjan, in Assam, enabling the China Air Task Force to guard the ferry and to strike at targets in Burma.

The American flyers were forced to employ superior tactics in order to survive combat with numerically superior forces. Fighter aircraft continued to operate in much the same manner as had the AVG, turning every advantage of the outmoded P-40's against the weaknesses of enemy planes. General Chennault drove home to his pilots the lessons he had learned from years of experience. With the advent of a handful of medium bombers in China, ingeniously devised methods of escort proved eminently successful.

The arrival of the first B-25's had been marred by tragedy. Early in June, 6 planes, under the command of Maj. Gordon Leland, left Dinjan for Kunming. Attempting to penetrate a solid cloud overcast at 10,000 feet, 3 of the aircraft, including that of Major Leland, crashed into a mountain and burned. A fourth plane ran out of gas, but its crew bailed out safely and reached their destination 2 weeks later. By this time 6 more B-25's had arrived at Kunming, bringing the new squadron commander, Maj. William E. Basye, who had flown a B-17 in the Java campaign, and 7 flyers who had participated in the Doolittle raid on Tokyo. One of the planes, permanently out of commission, provided spare parts which kept the remaining 7 B-25's in operation for almost 2 months.

Even before formal organization of the China Air Task Force, the medium bombers inaugurated their operations. On 1 July, 4 B-25's, escorted by 5 P-40's of the AVG, bombed harbor installations at Hankow, though with questionable results. A more successful attack was made on the following day. The Japanese immediately retaliated by sending 5 bombers over Hengyang airfield, but all bombs fell to the right of the landing strip. On 3 July the opposing forces again exchanged blows, the B-25's and P-40's striking at the large enemy-held airdrome at Nanchang, southeast of Hankow, and enemy forces bombing the Hengyang field with even less accuracy than on the previous attempt.

In line with a policy of reducing Japanese air power by bombing important bases, the B-25's on 4 July shifted their target southward to strike the Tien Ho Airdrome at Canton. After the five medium bombers and their fighter escort had bombed runways, parked aircraft, and the airdrome building without opposition, they headed for Kweilin, the advance base south of Hengyang. Here their landing was delayed for 15 minutes while the 23d Fighter Group tangled with new twin-engine fighters which the enemy had sent over the field. Members of the 23d Group had been practicing with the AVG during the previous weeks, and success of this initial combat on the very day of AVG induction indicated that the Japanese were to have no respite from American fighter planes.

Because of the excellent warning system which had been established by the Chinese with the aid of General Chennault, fighter planes had ample time to get into the most advantageous position for interception, and the Japanese were deprived of their chief weapon of surprise.

Enemy attacks were frequent and determined. On 30 July, for example, an estimated 119 bombers and fighters were sent over the American air base at Hengyang. Outnumbered members of the 23d Fighter Group engaged the attacking planes over a period of 36 hours, accounting for 17 enemy bombers and fighters with a loss of only 3 P-40's and no pilots.

Unfavorable weather, combat fatigue, exhausted supplies of bombs and fuel, and need for aircraft repairs frequently forced the American bombers into brief periods of inactivity. Such periods gave the airmen an opportunity to improve their weapons. Under the direction of Lt. Elmer Tarbox, twin .50-cal. machine guns were placed in the B-25 nose, twin .30-cal. guns were substituted for the bottom turret, and one .30-cal. gun was set up in the rear where it could be fired by either top or bottom gunner. The troublesome hand method of dropping fragmentation bombs was replaced by a bomb rack devised by Lt. Robert W. Roose. Such improvements made the B-25 a more useful weapon as the China Air Task Force enlarged the scope of its operations.

On 9 August, 5 B-25's and 3 P-40's attacked the important Indo-China port of Haiphong, marking the first time the task force had reached outside of China or Burma to hit the enemy. Before reaching the target the planes had to halt at an airfield only 5 minutes' flying time from enemy lines, while swarms of Chinese workmen refueled the aircraft out of 5-gallons cans. Results of the attack justified the risks involved and the efforts expended. A 4,000-ton freighter was sunk in the harbor, large fires which burned for 3 days were started in the dock and warehouse area, while direct bomb hits on Japanese headquarters caused a number of casualties variously estimated at from 100 to 400.

General Chennault's "hit and run" policy, dubbed guerrilla warfare by the Japanese, kept the enemy guessing as to where the next strike would be made. In the latter part of August the bombers were transferred to Yunnanyi in southwest China in order to bolster the Burma aerial campaign. During the last week of the month, the B-25's twice bombed Lashio, important rail center and air base; they crossed the border of Indo-China to attack enemy supply dumps at Hoang Su Phi and Phu Lo; and on the last 2 days of August they bombed Myitkyina, northernmost depot of the enemy in Burma.

Following this series of raids, the bombers returned to Hengyang and Kweilin, leaving Burmese operations during September and early October to the two B-25's and few fighters which had been stationed at Dinjan. The main part of the task force meantime carried out raids over occupied China, harassing shipping on inland waterways, disrupting rail communications, and destroying enemy aircraft on the ground and in the air. Early in October, however, the bombers turned their attention southward in order to aid the Chinese who were opposing renewed enemy attempts to cross the Salween River. Eleven missions were flown against enemy targets in northeast Burma, including supply depots at Tengchung, Mangshih, Wanling, Chefang, and Lichiapo.

India Air Task Force

The latest enemy push along the Salween coincided with the end of the monsoon season. Japanese aircraft were now expected to offer serious opposition to ferry operations, particularly along the western end of the route which terminated at Dinjan. The Tenth Air Force, charged with both operation and defense of the ferry, was barely in a position to carry out either task, although leasing of transport planes from the China National Airways Company had brought about some improvement in the air cargo service. In order to provide more effective defense of the ferry and to aid Chinese resistance along the Salween, General Bissell carried out his previous plan of organizing all American combat units in India as the India Air Task Force. The new organization was effected on 3 October, with Brig. Gen. Caleb V. Haynes as commander. Initial operational strength was almost negligible, for all three components, the 7th Bombardment Group, the 51st Fighter Group, and the recently activated 341st Bombardment Group (M), were far below their normal strength, either because of diversions to the Middle East and China or because of incomplete equipment.

Within a week the 26th Squadron and headquarters of the 51st Fighter Group were moved to Dinjan, giving the ferry a measure of protection. Efforts to set up an adequate air-warning system throughout Assam had met with little success, as the necessary equipment was not available. In the latter part of October, word was received that the Tenth Air Force would be relieved of its responsibility of operating the ferry, effective 1 December. The 1st Ferry Group was to be taken over by the Air Transport Command and Col. E. H. Alexander designated to head the India-China Wing of the ATC. But the Tenth Air Force was still charged with defending the aerial life-line to China, and before its meager forces could be deployed, the long-dreaded attack on Dinjan occurred. Approximately 100 enemy planes, equipped with belly tanks for the flight from the distant base at Lashio, on 25 October bombed and strafed Dinjan as well as newer airfields at Chabua, Mohanbari, and Sookerating. American forces received only a few minutes' warning and consequently suffered heavily. Five transports, 5 P-40's, and 2 P-43's were destroyed, while 4 transports and 13 fighters were badly damaged. Further attacks on 26 and 28 October were less damaging.

The aerial assaults at least served to emphasize the seriousness of the situation in Assam and added weight to General Bissell's request for the return of heavy bombers which had accompanied General Brereton to the Middle East. Crews of the experienced 9th Bombardment Squadron had already begun to arrive in India, bringing B-24's instead of the older B-17's which they flew to the Middle East in the summer. The planes were immediately put into action against suitable targets.

On 21 October the B-24's attacked power plants and pumping stations at Linsi in northern China, marking the first use of heavy bombers in China and the first strike by the AAF north of the Yangtse. The presence of the long-range Liberator in the CBI theater gave the Tenth Air Force a wider choice of targets and made it increasingly difficult for the enemy to predict where the next blows would fall. For several weeks, while the India Air Task Force was being built up, General Haynes employed his forces defensively with only occasional offensive missions by small flights of heavy bombers.

Later Operations

In China the task force under General Chennault continued its operations along the pattern followed in the summer, making carefully calculated attacks on lucrative targets and taking a heavy toll of enemy planes. The first medium bomber reinforcements had arrived on 5 October, increasing the bomber unit strength to 12 B-25's, 12 six-man crews, and 40 ground men. In their first night-bombing mission in China, the B-25's on 25 October demolished a power plant at Hong Kong, depriving the Japanese of electricity for shipyards where they repaired vessels damaged in the South Pacific fighting. Other targets in the area were hit earlier in the day by both bombers and fighters, destroying many of the dock installations and accounting for 20 of an estimated 21 enemy planes, with the loss of only 1 American fighter and 1 bomber—the first B-25 to be lost since the activation of the China Air Task Force.

Following attacks on the enemy airfield at Lashio on the 27th and 28th, the task force returned to hit the Kowloon Docks at Hong Kong, the fighter planes this time inaugurating dive bombing in the China theater. A period of routine activity was broken on 23 November by major strikes on the Indo-China port of Haiphong, the Tien Ho Airdrome at Canton, and air installations on Sanchu Island south of Canton. During the latter part of the month the task force also carried out a series of raids against Hankow, Yochow, and Sienning, to aid the Chinese who were attempting to repel an enemy push across the Sintsiang River near Yochow.

On 27 November General Chennault assembled 10 bombers and 23 fighters—the largest number of planes ever used in a single operation in China up to that time. The force carried out a successful attack on Hong Kong shipping, dock installations, and warehouses. In 4 days the task force had destroyed more than 60 enemy planes on the ground and in the air.

By this time the India Air Task Force had been sufficiently reinforced to broaden the scope of its activity. Small flights of bombers had successfully attacked Rangoon on 5 and 9 November. Shifting of the 25th Fighter Squadron from Karachi to Sookerating late in October had increased the size of flights on strafing sweeps, and rapid development of the P-40 as a bomber had enabled the force to inflict greater damage on targets within range.

On 20 November Col. C. F. Necrason led 8 B-24's in a damaging attack on the marshalling yards at Mandalay, initiating an air offensive against Burma and Thailand which was destined to last for more than 6 months. On the 26th of the month 9 B-24's of the 9th and 436th Squadrons, again led by Colonel Necrason, took off from Gaya and flew a round trip of 2,760 miles in a surprise attack on an oil refinery and power plant at Bangkok, Thailand. The dangerously long mission was repeated 1 month later by 12 B-24's.

These and similar missions were in addition to the routine "milk run" to Rangoon, where the long-range bombers regularly attacked harbor installations and shipping. The B-24's invariably had to fly without fighter escort, but losses were slight. The P-40 fighter-bombers continued to hit targets in northern and central Burma. From 20 November to 31 December the entire India Air Task Force dropped only

198 tons of bombs. But there was evidence that the Tenth Air Force was gaining aerial ascendancy in the China-Burma-India theater. After reinforcements were rushed to airfields in Assam in October and November, the Japanese failed to follow up their successful attacks of late October. Instead, late in December the enemy countered with a series of bombing assaults on Calcutta and Chittagong and on airdromes at Dum Dum, Alipore, Fenny, and Yunnanyi, indicating perhaps that the Japanese believed the American bombing missions were being flown from these fields. In an effort to forestall these blows, the China Air Task Force threw its weight against enemy airfields and supply dumps in Burma during the last 2 weeks of December.

As the year came to a close, the Tenth Air Force was still short of the 252 planes allotted the preceding June, but in personnel strength the force had reached a total of 10,316 officers and men—almost double the size of the force 6 months earlier. While the Tenth was not yet in a position to undertake large-scale operations, it had survived a crucial period in the CBI theater. Many of the difficulties incidental to initial operations in a strange land had now been overcome or alleviated. The Karachi Air Base was well established as a reception, classification, and training center for men arriving in India. The service command, having established depots and bases across India and in China, was better able to supply and maintain combat units.

Despite the limited scale of operations, the air task forces in China and India had proved equal to the dual job of protecting the vital air transport line and of taking offensive action against enemy targets in Burma, China, Thailand, and Indo-China. Superior tactics and a keen sense of urgency had enabled a small air force to challenge Japanese supremacy in the most remote zone of American combat.

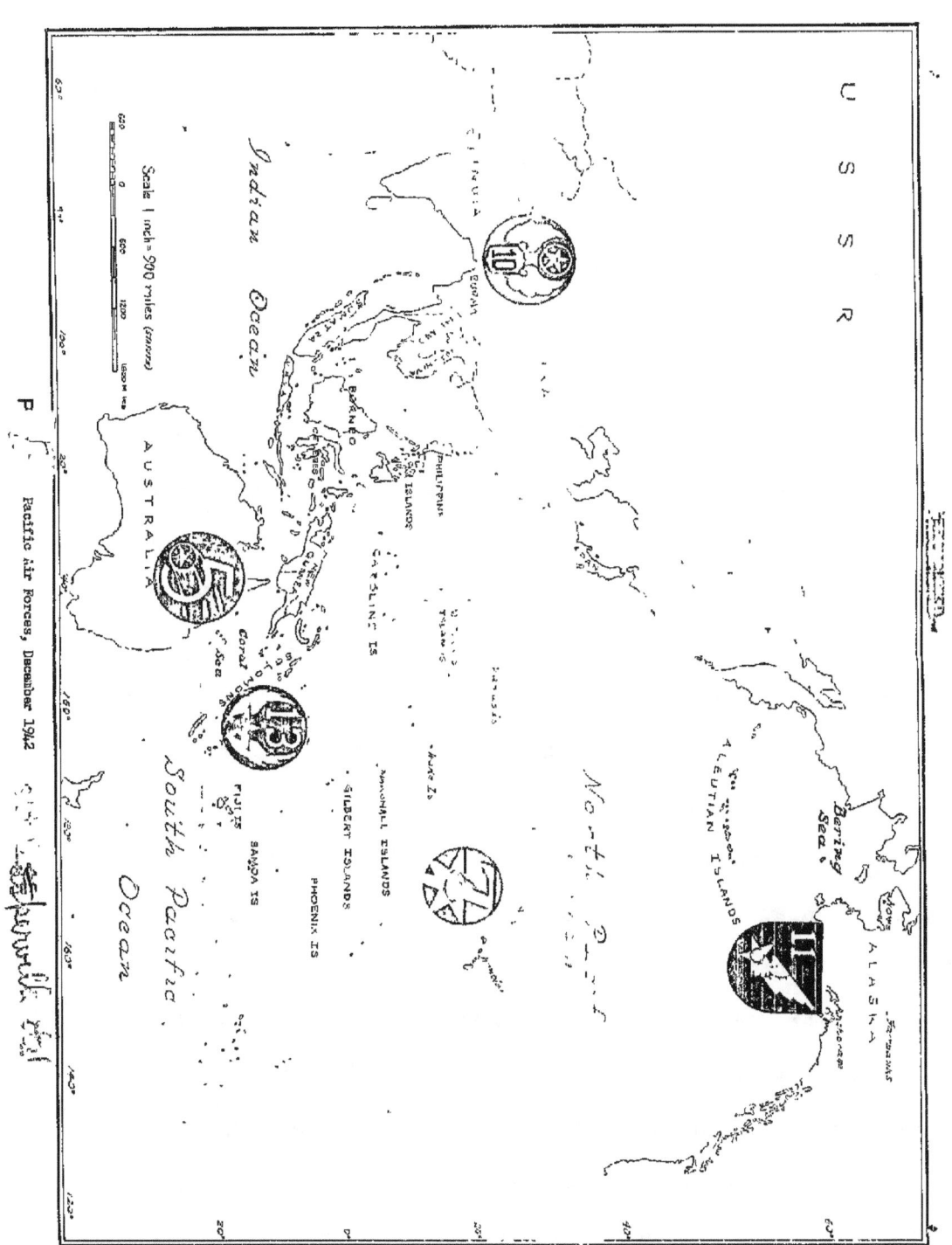

Pacific Air Forces, December 1942

EPILOGUE

This then was the record of Army Air forces in the first phase of the war against Japan.

Subsequent years brought a series of Allied successes which stemmed from the limited offensives of late 1942. Following a withdrawal of Japanese forces from Guadalcanal in February 1943, the Allies used their Solomons springboard for further moves and within 6 months the line of advance had reached Rendova and New Georgia in the Central Solomons. Early in November a third step placed American forces on Bougainville, which offered the Thirteenth Air Force and Marine units a base only 215 nautical miles from Rabaul. While aircraft concentrated on neutralization of this stronghold in New Britain, other advances were made in the Northern Solomons and into the Bismarck Archipelago. During February and March 1944, landings in the Admiralty and St. Matthais islands placed Allied aircraft astride the supply line to Rabaul, and the Solomons offensive had technically reached its conclusion.

The Fifth Air Force, having contributed to the reduction of Rabaul and to Allied occupation of southwestern New Britain, now directed its full strength westward in New Guinea. By the end of 1943 the Huon Gulf area, including Lae, Salamaua, Finschaven, had come under Allied control, and within 7 months the Fifth had advanced through Wakde, Biak, and Noemfoor to the Cape Sansapor area, the farthest limit of western New

Guinea. In June 1944 the Fifth and Thirteenth Air Forces were formally united under the Far East Air Forces, preparatory to the drive for the Philippines. Invasion of Morotai in the Halmaheras on 15 September was followed by the culminating step of Southwest Pacific operations—invasion of the Philippines, which occurred with the Leyte landings on 20 October 1944. Success on Leyte permitted the advance to Mindoro in December and to Luzon in January.

These moves toward the Philippines had been coordinated with a Central Pacific offensive, which had brought the Seventh Air Force into active combat in the autumn of 1943. A November invasion of Tarawa, Apemama, and Makin in the Gilbert Islands was followed by seizure of the Marshall atolls of Kwajalein and Majuro in January 1944. Within a month Eniwetok was taken, and the Marianas loomed as the next objective. June and July brought the invasion of Saipan and Guam, enabling units of the Seventh Air Force to move to bases within striking distance of the Bonin and Volcano islands.

In the North Pacific the Aleutian campaign had been concluded with American occupation of Attu in May 1943 and of Kiska in August. Eleventh Air Force bombers were thus brought into position for strikes against Japan's Kurile Islands.

On the Asiatic mainland the Fourteenth Air Force, formed from the China Air Task Force in March 1943, and the Tenth Air Force, still located in India, continued to hit the Japanese in Burma and China. Newly-arrived B-24's enabled the Fourteenth to inaugurate operations against shipping in the China Sea in mid-1943.

The long-awaited appearance of the B-29 Superfortress came on 15 June 1944, with the China-based XX Bomber Command's attack on Yawata, Japanese steel center on the island of Kyushu. The Marianas-based XXI Bomber Command, second component of the Twentieth Air Force, made its announced debut on 24 November 1944 in a Superfortress attack on Tokyo. Following the early experimental operations, the B-29's attacked strategic targets in the Japanese home islands with a steadily-increasing force.

Three and a half years after the forced withdrawal of B-17's from Clark Field and Del Monte, Philippine bases had been recaptured, and additional bases secured in China, the Ryukyus, Marianas, and Volcanos; fleets of 500 Superfortresses were repeatedly saturating the Japanese homeland with incendiary attacks; and AAF units were moving from the European theater for the final assault on Japan. With Army air force commanders in the Pacific announcing the planned employment of still newer types of aircraft, the air war against Japan promised to surpass in speed and intensity every comparable effort in World-War-II.

www.ingramcontent.com/pod-product-compliance
Lightning Source LLC
Chambersburg PA
CBHW082120230426
43671CB00015B/2755